★☆★☆★☆★☆★☆★

Zickary
Zan

★☆★☆★☆★☆★☆★

★☆☆★☆★☆★☆★☆★☆★☆★☆★

Zickary Zan

★☆☆★☆★☆★☆★☆★☆★☆★☆★

CHILDHOOD
FOLKLORE
COMPILED BY
JACK
AND
OLIVIA
SOLOMON

ILLUSTRATIONS BY MARK BREWTON

THE UNIVERSITY OF ALABAMA PRESS

UNIVERSITY, ALABAMA

Library of Congress Cataloging in Publication Data
Main entry under title:

Zickary Zan.

 Bibliography: p.
 Includes index.
 1. Folk-lore—Alabama. 2. Folk-lore and children—
Alabama. 3. Games—Alabama. I. Solomon, Jack,
1927-   II. Solomon, Olivia, 1937-
GR110. A2Z48   398.8′09761   79-1117
ISBN 0-8173-0012-0

Contents

Preface

In the spring of 1970 we happened on a strange and beautiful volume called . . . *I never saw another butterfly,** a collection of poems, drawings, and paintings by children in Terezin concentration camp, 1942–1944, not far from Prague. It is a book that ought to change the entire course of history. Of the 15,000 children under the age of fifteen who entered Terezin, perhaps 100 survived. Their words and pictures should burn our hates and cruelties so purely that not even the ashes would sift through the air of a new heaven and a new earth where the bright hope of the child is all. Look for a moment at their drawings: a sturdy boatman astride his small burnt-umber craft in a landscape of gray-green sea and fishes; a sunny garden landscape dominated by a bright yellow house; a blue-ink grandfather, long bearded, hair flying, eyes wild and sharp; rows of red-roofed houses; a church, mournful in the grays and browns of dusk; a single barred window, gold in the sunshine; a pencil sketch of a small boy against a great fence; a row of dormitory beds; the endless train of the deported; a tiny SS figure; everywhere flowers and trees; a single deep-green leaf; the imprint of a child's hand; the children themselves, lined up for bread, holding hands as if in a dance or game, wandering in wood and field, jumping rope, and, yes, the butterfly! Hear them speak:

> *No, no, my God, we want to live! . . .*
> *I loved you once. Goodbye, my love! . . .*
> *Listen! . . .*
> *Now it's time. . . .*

Those are the voices of the children of Terezin. The rhymes, riddles, and games in this book are the voices of the children of Alabama. Wherever we have honored and nurtured the child with all our strength, there have we achieved greatness; wherever we have abused and exploited, killed a sweet body and tender spirit, there have we descended to infamy. The inconceivable shame of child mass murder—there may be no atonement for innocence outraged, enslaved, slaughtered. *Zickary Zan* is an indictment of such evil. Let the heart exult in the high joy of these pages. Let us understand clearly what is here: the one perfect symbol of transfiguration, a child at play.

The first volume of this series in Alabama folklore, *Cracklin Bread and Asfidity*, is a collection of remedies and recipes, folk traditions

---

* . . . *I never saw another butterfly: Children's Drawings and Poems from Terezin Concentration Camp 1942–1944*, edited by Hana Volavkova. English translation by Jeanne Neumcova. New York: McGraw-Hill Book Company, published in a special edition by the State Museum in Prague, 1962.

associated largely with the home. Alabama folk life exhibits four well-defined centers: the home, the school, the store, and the church. Though arbitrary classifications of any subject are never completely satisfactory, especially in the study of folklore, which ranges over the entire mind and heart of man, and while it is extremely difficult to determine the precise sources and circumstances of folk transmission, we can assign most American folklore generally to one of these four centers. *Zickary Zan* is a collection of that Alabama folklore assimilated, shared, and transmitted primarily in the school. It includes folk games, game songs and rhymes, riddles, proverbs, nonsense verse, parodies, counting-out chants, taunts, and autograph verse. Folk songs and tales are also transmitted in the school, but we have encountered such an extraordinary volume of Alabama folk songs and tales that we cannot present them here. And, admittedly, some of the folk items in *Zickary Zan* are learned first in the home from brothers and sisters, parents and grandparents, and relatives and friends.

For the most part, however, *Zickary Zan* is strongly tied to the school. Constructed early in the history of a community, soon after the church and the store, the American schoolhouse served not only as a living repository of oral folklore but also as the actual site of various folk gatherings: political rallies, barbecues, traveling entertainments, dances, and play parties. And to a great extent folk life and lore still find a center in the school—in homecoming, athletic events, graduation, proms, Halloween carnivals, and spring festivals. Here, as in the church, the home, and the store, our folk traditions continue, nourished every day by the fresh waters of youth. It is, perhaps, too much to hope that every school system in the state of Alabama would set about writing its history, consulting both the public documents and personal letters, diaries, old sketches and photographs, and memories of elderly citizens. Yet, that is what ought to be done. Looking back can teach us what is now and what is to come.

As parents and teachers we have spent most of our lives with children. We live directly across the street from the school—handsome, early twentieth-century brick buildings—within sight and sound of a thousand children. It is pleasure and mystery to watch them come and go, to enter the doors of a world we left but remember. Which of us can forget the stiff new overalls and hard squeaking shoes, the clean paper and unsharpened pencil of the magical first day of school? Like the castles of our fairy tales, the schoolhouse itself is enchanted. Dragons, ogres, wizards, brave knights and beautiful damsels, tournaments to the death, and high, shining celebrations—all wait for the children who will enter a realm where they will prove themselves or shatter their dreams. And though there may be no gigantic tree on the playground and the teacher no longer rings a cast-iron bell, even the sleekest concrete and glass structure exerts over us an odd power.

All our efforts at teaching the child are based on what we—educators, psychologists, teachers, administrators—think school is, not on how the child sees school. If we but stirred our memories a bit, we might walk in the door with the child—re-experience those rites of passage, the intimacy of friendships never again equaled in all our lives: the humiliation of a scolding, the grin of wickedness caught in the act and delivered unto justice, the snubbing of a nose bloodied in a fair fight, the flushed cheeks of the victor ashamed of his victory, the quick, courageous rescue of a weaker playfellow from a bully, the pressure of a knee on cold ground, the thumb poised just so against an

aggie, the swinging of rope in hot pease, the pencil clutched tightly, the number eight, the letter J scrawling miraculously into form and meaning, the equation transformed into hieroglyphics before one's very eyes, the poem into something like cuneiform, the answer gone into oblivion. Who among us cannot remember the very spot where we sneaked a kiss or swore the oath of blood brothers?

The folklore in this collection is widely circulated throughout the United States, Anglo-American in tradition, yet peculiarly Southern, rural, and small town in its emphases, flavor, and the preservation of certain centuries-old items. We insist that *Zickary Zan* is not a slice of nostalgia, not a collection of quaint museum or curio pieces, but rather a dynamic lore still in the active possession and use of Alabama folk, still transmitted orally and in practice by children to children, and by adults to children. It is true that some of the games are not widely popular or have undergone various transformations, some rhymes and riddles have passed or are passing out of folk circulation, and the autograph album itself and its language have given way to high school annuals; but their spirit survives in a thousand ways. What is remarkable is not the loss of a few games or chants, but the continuation of a great body of folk materials. Equally astounding is the coexistence of a predominantly rural, small-town folklore, that often can be traced back for two hundred and fifty years, with the primarily urban, technological folklore of contemporary media, which just as often as it creates new folk traditions draws on and reinforces the older ones.

The bulk of this collection—folk games, riddles, taunts, proverbs, and rhymes—is derived from field investigations conducted by students at Troy State University, from 1958 to 1962. Some of the riddles were collected by Ruby Pickens Tartt in Sumter County, Alabama, as part of the national WPA folklore researches made during the 1930s; the Schoolteachers' Diary, from Tallapoosa County, Alabama, has been edited from the original manuscript now in the possession of Mr. Jacob Walker, Opelika, Alabama; the two autograph albums were given to us by Mrs. Ruth Herren and Mrs. Ruth Hornsby, both of Tallassee, Alabama. We are grateful to Mr. Walker, Mrs. Herren, and Mrs. Hornsby for their kind permission to include them here.

Because *Zickary Zan* tells us about the child and the school, about our social history and folk life, we trust that the teacher, the psychologist, the historian, and the folklorist will find much to ponder here. Chiefly, though, we hope that parents, grandparents, and children will read this book, for they are its makers. Here, for your delight and memory are the oft-cited proverbs that fell about our ears at the slightest provocation, the riddles and taunts we exchanged on the way home, the games we played in dusty, muddy schoolyards, the Latin exercises we struggled over on a cold day, the words sweethearts and friends inscribed in albums of friendship. Here are Old Molly Rier, William Trembletoe, Hickory Ben Double, Cinderella, the Spanish Dancer, Billy Booster, Buster Brown, Old Aunt Pearly and Lula Belle, the fiddling sow, the lady with the alligator purse, and a host of other old friends.

Listen, now, to the voices of the children of Alabama. We offer them as a memorial to the slain children of Terezin and of all this earth.

> Here I stand
> All ragged and dirty,
> If you don't come and kiss me,
> I'll run like a turkey!

★★★★★★★★★★★

Zickary
Zan

★★★★★★★★★★★

Introduction

We are glad that *Cracklin Bread and Asfidity* made readers happy. As we had hoped, it stirred memories of home and evoked pride in our rich, varied Alabama folk heritage. One aspect of reader response especially impressed us; everywhere people are eager to tell us of their own personal experience with folk remedies and recipes. One says his mama used asfidity to wean her numerous children, another describes how grandma made *her* poultices, and one lady gave us some asfidity a half century old. Again and again we encounter "Have you got in there about so-and-so?" or "Bet you haven't got this one!" or "I've had a many-a dose of that stuff." Kind neighbors made us real gingerbread, real cracklin bread, real buttermilk pie, and one fellow dug red sassafras for a marvelous tea.

All of us share in a broad collective folk consciousness; we grow around and into the tales, songs, riddles, games, superstitions, and sayings of our folk community, and yet, despite this common background, any folklore item will, ultimately, bear a personal signature. Each of us has his own way—you count potatoes, I say eeny-meeny-miny-mo; you play hopscotch with one double-block, I play it with two; you chant "All hid? Is you all hid," I chant "Who ain't hid can't hide over!" You put in the nutmeg, I leave it out. And although there exist common denominators that a folklorist can identify in a body of national, regional, or local folklore, themes that recur in world-wide mythology, behind every variant of a riddle, a rhyme, a tale, or a song there is a real, live human being to whom that particular expression was or is meaningful. The lore has no existence without the folk.

The transmission and assimilation of folklore occur within specific, personal circumstances, and we cannot discount this truth in our efforts to formulate a methodology and a philosophy of folklore as a subject of serious inquiry. From the very beginning folklorists have been bedeviled and plagued by critics who variously charged, often acrimoniously and condescendingly, that folklore was trivial, unfit for scholarly investigation, and lowbrow, that its methods were irresponsible, and the results ludicrous. Remedies, superstitions, and folk beliefs were the afflictions of abysmally ignorant, uneducated clods in whom the light of rational intellect shone not at all; folk rhymes and verses were debased, corrupt doggerel; folk customs were vestigial remains of savage rites; folk songs, save for the ballads enshrined in print by respectable authors, were sentimental, obscene, morbid, or tasteless, their music, primitive or, at best, quaintly charming; folk tales were the vulgar oral traditions of people who could not read, and, if these stories ever got in print, totally deficient in literary value. In short, the whole thing was disreputable, and those who pursued it were the lunatic fringe. It is a wonder that folklore collectors did not pack their bags for the bush. That they did not and kept at it, defying their detractors, defending both their methods and the value of folklore studies, is a tribute to their moral and intellectual courage, their dedication to the folk, and the vigor and endurance of the folk mind. Some of them even lived to see their years of diligent study rewarded by extremely tardy, and often grudging, recognition. Unhappily, folklore scholars still feel, to this very day, the need to defend their study, their methods, and the folk.

In the light of this curious state of affairs, we offer some comments about the collecting and editing of materials in *Zickary Zan*, which, like *Cracklin Bread and Asfidity*, grew out of an introductory folklore course in the English Department at Troy State University, 1958 to 1962. The objectives of the course were simple: defining folklore, introducing a basic system of classification, and experience in field research. Most of the students went home on the weekends, and home was the small towns and rural communities of central and southeastern Alabama. From Friday afternoon until Sunday night, Troy State students interviewed their families, friends, and neighbors. All students collected items in all categories—games, rhymes, riddles, place names, superstitions, remedies, recipes, epitaphs, tales, and songs. However, often in the course of their field studies, a particular emphasis would emerge, either out of personal preference or because a given geographical area might be richer in one genre than in another. Occasionally, a student collector would work up a folklore/folk-life profile of some community. Every single item, whether a folk tale or a proverb, was entered on a separate sheet of paper; the name, address, age, and any other pertinent biographical data of the informant of that item appeared on the reverse side of the page. Collection efforts were severely hampered by the lack of funds for any equipment, especially the camera and tape recorder. A few students fortunately owned or had access to either one or the other, so that, over a decade, we had a fair sampling of folk songs and some photographs. Student collectors were carefully instructed in the matter of authentic transcription of materials from informants; in the collection of the folk tales especially, they were urged to take down the story in the language of the speaker, not re-create it in their own words. Now and then, the informant himself would write out the words and musical notation for a song, a recipe, instructions for a craft, or a folk tale.

Because of the absence of cameras and tape recorders, folk-life studies were extremely limited in the Troy State years, but the class as a whole made several short journeys to local cemeteries, to Perry's Store in Kinston, Alabama, and to Tatum Bedsole's museum in

Hacoda, Alabama. The folklore course was climaxed every spring with a fair (and in those days such festivals were rare) on the quadrangle— the exhibition of folk artifacts, ranging from needlework to farm implements, of folk crafts like quilting, folk games like sack races, and greased pig chases, folk singers, and a dance with music by those fine folk musicians, the Rushin family of Shellhorn, Alabama.

Troy State students took to all this demonstration of their heritage like the proverbial ducks to water; the course in folklore was not only highly successful in the collection of field data but also extremely popular: it was easy, it was fun, there was plenty of it out there for everybody, and, once the wellsprings of their own folk traditions were tapped, they were excited and pleased to learn that all that "stuff" possessed meaning and worth. They went through all sorts of gaps, from the literal one in the fence to those between generations, neighborhoods, families, religions, and economic and social milieus. In those actual face-to-face encounters with their parents, relatives, neighbors, and strangers, they made new friends, renewed and deepened old ties and bonds, and came to look on their personal, community, state, and regional history in a new, clearer light. Not the least of their accomplishments was the abandonment of the shreds of every kind of arrogance, condescension, and shame, the birth of pride in their folk heritage, the attributes of a civilized, rational, and responsible person, humor, sincerity, gratitude, tact, patience, and painstaking discipline. The course did for them what it does for any collector: they began to know who they were, where they lived, and what for. By now there is a network of all those students and informants throughout Alabama, and it has been our joy to preserve their work and their heritage of folklore in these volumes.

The first step in editing those field studies conducted by Troy State students among three to four thousand informants in the counties of Escambia, Butler, Wilcox, Conecuh, Barber, Lowndes, Geneva, Dale, Coffee, Covington, Crenshaw, Pike, Bullock, Elmore, Montgomery, and Tallapoosa was the collation of manuscripts. Next, exact duplicates were eliminated; all significant variants were retained. What was "significant" may have been only a few words, but those words altered meaning, imparted a different flavor, or offered another dimension of folk life. The choices for inclusion of variants in *Zickary Zan* were most delicate because the items themselves appear to be so small. In *Cracklin Bread*, the folk remedies were so numerous, and often so similar that, again, the tasks of selection, arrangement, and presentation were difficult; the recipes, however, usually possessed marked individuality, although some of them, for example, those for pound cake and tea cakes, were reported by a hundred or more different informants and nearly all exhibited some subtle difference from the others. Editing folk tales and folk songs is far less complicated: the song and its variants belong to one singer, though one singer may know many songs and one song may exist in several different versions in any one community; the tales exhibit similar motifs, but every tale has its own voice and its own structure.

The methodology of folklore field research requires wide sampling and the citation of all important variants. We have, therefore, included many variants that will appear to be redundant or inconsistent. Consider, for example, the following two entries that appear to be quite similar; an oral reading, however, will quickly establish measurable differences in rhythm:

> Bluebelle, cockleshells, evy, ivy, over
>
> . . . .
>
> Blue bells, cockshells, evy-wy-o.

The nursery-rhyme character William Trimbletoe appears in *Zickary Zan* as *Tremble Toe, tremble toe, Tremble toe,* and *Trimbletoe;* the variant spellings subtly alter meaning, image (the wonderfully comic trembling toe), and rhythm. In general, whenever the editors speak, spelling is regularized according to current usage in other folklore and nursery-rhyme anthologies, but the spelling actually submitted or reported by the original informant is preserved in the texts. Hence, both *Lulabelle* and *Lula Belle,* both *Moly* and *Molly,* both *Farmer* and *Farmer's,* both *Merry* and *Mary.* Similarly, there are several spellings of *eeny-meeny-mo, teddy bear,* and *icky-bicky.* Sometimes variant spellings, as in hot *pease* and *peas,* require an explanation, which is given in a note. Punctuation is supplied in the texts whenever clarity and logic demand, with the exception of the autograph albums and the Schoolteachers' Diary, all of which exist in manuscript and which we have transcribed as faithfully as we could.

In some cases, inconsistencies are explained by usage and function: the frog-in-the-millpond verse appears both as a taunt and as a song to accompany a game; a folk game played with bat and ball is *Mumbally Peg* while the knife game is *Mumble Peg* or *Mumbely Peg.* In other cases, sense or emotional quality may call for the inclusion of variants: "Kiss me quick / and I'll run like a turkey!" is not quite the same as "If you don't come and kiss me / I'll run like a turkey!" Again, variant spelling and punctuation may indicate geographical preference—one of our oldest Anglo-American counting-out rhymes is reported in four variants where differences in both meaning and rhythm are apparent:

> Wire, briar, limber lock   . . .   Wild briar, limbralock
>
> Wild briar, limbra lock   . . .   Wire, brier, limber lock

In all those instances, and in many more not cited here, we have been guided by the methodology and practice of other editors of folklore collections.

Two of the most important canons of folklore scholarship are the presentation of findings exactly as they exist and are reported and the accurate identification of sources and informants. Unfortunately, the role of the folklorist as reliable reporter and his stern commitment to intellectual honesty may conflict with his moral responsibility. This is the case with the word *nigger* in many of the rhymes reported by informants to both the student collectors and the editors. Up until two decades ago the word was routinely reported in nearly all printed collections without apology or explanation. At this moment the word is in wide usage among the folk, even as Polack jokes are all the rage in oral folk humor. Keeping in mind that the rhyme texts of *Zickary Zan* began to be collected twenty years ago, we can report that our recent studies indicate that the frequency of usage is declining rapidly among children; in fact *nigger* has almost been expunged on the playground with *tiger* and *rabbit* dominating the acceptable substitutes. Verbal obscenities are more widespread in contemporary American folklore than ethnic jokes, quips, and slurs; no obscenities were reported to us, and if they had been, they should have emphatically been excluded here in this volume, which we hope children will enjoy. Our last survey of the verbal folklore current among high school students did not turn up a single profane or obscene utterance. In short, we pitted the folklorist against the parent and teacher, and the folklorist lost. Because of those ethical and moral considerations, we also rejected one anti-Semitic taunt. Therefore, please note the deletion of the word *nigger* and the substitution *fellow*. We do not wish to contribute to the preservation of that term, among either children or adults, through these pages.

As in *Cracklin Bread and Asfidity*, the informants of the items in *Zickary Zan* were primarily white, middle-class residents of central and southeastern Alabama. They represent all the ordinary occupations of Alabama folk from farmer and garage mechanic to homemaker, secretary, and teacher. A few were octogenarians, many were children, some were high school students, and many were adults in mid-life. The bulk of the collection was reported by Troy State University students, the editors gathered some items from friends, neighbors, and relatives, and several of the folk games were collected by Alexander City State Junior College students, 1972–1979. Though we made no attempts at statistical analysis, our readers will be interested in knowing that reportings for any single item, with the obvious exception of manuscripts, were numerous. To all those givers, the student collectors and the informants, the editors say thank you.

Of all the qualities of folklore, the ones that have struck us most forcibly since the appearance of *Cracklin Bread and Asfidity* are its endless variety and its endurance. There is simply no way to eradicate it, and just when you think a folk item has vanished, it pops back up somewhere. The *Asfidity* part of our title stirred up arguments about spelling, uses, and one tale which somebody tells us everywhere we go. The teller swears to veracity; he names people, places, and dates, assuring us it all happened in his own hometown. It goes something like this: A fellow enters a general store, walks up to the clerk, and says, "I want a nickel's worth of asfidity." The clerk obliges, the customer says "Charge it to Foster Cunningham Thames." The clerk writes, scratches it out, writes some more, chews on his pencil, then finally bursts out, "Just go on and take it. I'm not about to spell Foster Cunningham Thames *and* asfidity for a nickel."

And so it went in Eclectic, Luverne, Goshen, Rutledge, Greenville, Enterprise, Andalusia, Opp, Red Hill, Equality, and Flea Hop. And so it goes on in *Zickary Zan* and among the folk of Alabama.

★☆★☆★★☆★★☆★★★☆

Folk
Play

★☆★☆★★☆★★☆★★★☆

Games

The folk games of children do not survive as mere half-forgotten remnants in the memories of old people. They have come down to us intact. Nor need we fear that they will soon pass out of existence. It is nothing short of remarkable to stand on an elementary-school playground and watch twentieth-century first graders chant, "Ring-around-the-rosy guinea, guinea, all squat!" No matter that they do not know what a guinea is; they know that, when the leader gives the signal, they sit down, and that the last to sit is either out of the game or pays the forfeit—tells the name of a sweetheart. At dusk the familiar cry is still raised: "Bushel of wheat, Bushel of rye, Who's not ready, Holler I!" or a childish corruption: "Butcherree, Butchrye, Who ain't ready, Holler I!" The folklorist may well puzzle over this continuing popularity.

Why are these games known and played by thousands of children when a ballad like "Barbara Allen" is remembered by only a few unless, of course, a popular singer has resurrected it? A few tentative answers may be suggested: (1) The folk game is learned and perpetuated in a group, and this learning is reinforced by hundreds of repetitions over a period of several years. (2) What we experience as children is often more vividly recollected than our other memories. (3) The simplicity of a folk game, the ease with which it is learned, its freedom from encumbrances, except the most common and readily available—a rock, a piece of glass or cloth, a rope, or a stick to draw lines in the dirt—all these favor its survival. Unhampered by complicated rules and equipment, utilizing only basic skills that nearly every child possesses, the folk game approaches the ideal in amusement and pleasure. And though, as in all games, the race is to the swift, the tug-of-war to the strong, the loser is rarely humiliated. The worst that can happen to a player is a good-natured taunt or being the last one called when the players choose up sides. The idea is not to win, but to play, a notion that could stand a bit more stress in an era where athletic competition is so fierce, even on the elementary level, as to be sometimes physically and emotionally damaging to children.

Traditional games like "London Bridge" and "Hide-and-Go-Seek" go far beyond winning and losing; though the child learns rudimentary social behavior in these early contests, it is the sheer delight in play, the exuberance and joy in one's own body, the fellowship of playmates, most aptly symbolized by the linked hands of circling dances, that strikes us. It is true that they learn to play by rules, to honor the rule (though arguments frequently break out over what the rule is and who violated it, how, when, and where), but the rules are few and the penalties light—usually naming a sweetheart—an important point for students of child development. And the age at which children abandon this folk play for organized sports and table-top games of checkers and cards is also significant. Their physical and intellectual growth is, of course, a determinant; yet there is another, more profound reason, one that gives us a yearning regret. Something of the spirit of childhood is forever lost. Call it what you will— innocence, magic, the natural unspoiled joy of youth—it is gone, never to be recaptured except in memory and the pattern of the game itself, the everlasting archetype of play.

The folk games we collected may be loosely categorized as: circling dances, often accompanied by song, like "We're Marching Round the Levee," "The Farmer in the Dell," "Ring around the Rosy," "Here We Go Loop-dy-Loo," and "Little Sally Walker"; line games such as "Red Rover, Red Rover," and "Bum, Bum, Bum, Here We Come"; chase games of which "Molly, Molly Bright" and "Hide-and-Go-Seek" are prototypes; combinations of circling and chase, notably "Drop-the-Handkerchief" and "Froggie in the Millpond"; pantomimes, the most famous of which is "Here We Go Round the Mulberry Bush"; progressive games, among which "May I," "Red Light," and "Rock School" are most widely popular; tumbling games such as "Pop the Whip," "Stiff Starch," and "Sling the Statues"; and tug-of-war, the most popular example being "London Bridge."

Certain games create their own categories. Hopscotch is a game of two skills, hopping and accurate throwing; its requisite diagram, drawn on the earth or sidewalk, links it to other board games with more extensive playing area—football, basketball, and baseball. "Mumble Peg" is played with pocketknives, a common enough object for schoolboys of the last century, now outlawed by most school authorities. "Club Fist," similar to the counting-out rhyme, "One Potato, Two Potato," is unique in the lengthy dialogue it involves (reminiscent of the "House That Jack Built" cumulative-dependency rhyme in Mother Goose) and the severity of its penalties. A descendant of "Club Fist" is the adolescent kissing game "This, That, and the Other," in which a player is blindfolded and asked "Who are you going to do this to?" as the questioner pantomimes a kiss, hug, or slap, whereupon the player must perform the action on the person whose name he called. Marbles has been played almost since man stood erect, only to get down on all fours again when he devised the game. The history of teaching is replete with records of confiscated aggies, and "to play for keeps" has become a byword in our language. Billiards is its more complex adult counterpart. Girls still play jackstones—not a toy counter in America is without them—but good steel jacks and a real rubber ball are hard to come by nowadays. Jacks are manufactured in plastic or aluminum, and the balls may be synthetic "super balls." Fifty years ago the game was often played with small pebbles, as it was during World War II, when steel was a nationalized defense product. "Pease Porridge Hot" is an ancient hand-clapping game, originally designed to warm a child's hands; the pattern of clapping varies in different locations.

Games played with infants and very young children are practically the same as they were three hundred years ago. Among the ones we collected are these favorites:

Patta-Cake

The adult holds the baby's hands in his, claps them, and says:

> Patta-cake, Patta-cake
> A baker's man,
> Make me a cake (or biscuit)
> As fast as you can.

Then he rolls the baby's hands over and over:

> Roll him over,
> Roll him over,

And lightly pushes the hands to baby's tummy:

> Throw him in the pan!

Horsey

The adult takes the child on his knees, clasps his hands, jiggles his legs up and down in a rhythm imitative of a horse's trot as he says:

> Ride a little horsey
> Down town.
> Watch out, horsey!

Suddenly he releases the child, allowing him to fall halfway through his legs:

> Don't fall down!

But quickly he retrieves baby and the game begins all over again. The adult may vary the point at which he allows the child to slip through his legs in order to add a pleasurable element of suspense.

An unusual rhyme to accompany "Horsey" was recently reported to us by Mrs. Luverne Hornsby of Tallassee, Alabama:

> Old horsey, keep your tail up.
> Old horsey, keep your tail up.
> And let the sun shine in!

"This Little Piggy," played with baby's toes, surely must be a national tradition, far better known than one finger game we collected, an Alabama version of several in Mother Goose:

> Little One,
> Ring One,
> Long One,
> Lick Pot,
> Thumbo.

Another finger game that fascinates small children is:

> There's the church,
> And there's the steeple,
> Open the door,
> And there are the people.

"Rooster, Pullet, and Hen" is really a practical joke played on children. The adult points to the eyes and names them "rooster," to the nose and says "pullet," to the chin and says "hen." Then he questions the child: "What did I say this was?" When he gets to the nose and the child answers "pullet," the questioner does just that—pulls it. A similar game involves pulling the nose and taunting, "Got your nose, got your nose." The nose is the thumb protruding from behind two fingers, but the child invariably will reach up to feel if his nose is still there. A much more cruel version is played by children with other children: The forefingers of the right hand are laid across the forefingers of the left, forming a chicken coop. The child is instructed to feed corn to the chickens. When he places his finger into the lattice "coop," the other child pinches it hard.

Play has social, intellectual, and emotional dimensions; and certainly, educators, sociologists, and psychologists may profitably examine the subject for revelations about the development, behavior, and learning patterns of children. While it is true, as Brian Sutton-Smith suggests in his essay, "Folk Games of Children" (Coffin, *Our Living Traditions*, New York, 1968), that these games have undergone a good many changes, most particularly the courtship games of adolescence, their essential structure has not altered and it is, rather, their universality and antiquity that are most striking. The captured prisoner in "London Bridge" may be a vestigial reminder of the ancient human sacrifice required at the dedication of a bridge, and circling around the mulberry bush is likely a survival of a spring fertility rite. Some of our earliest pictorial representations of children depict them in just such games as we have collected—with sticks, balls, ropes, hoops, and pebbles, leaping, hopping, giving chase, and dancing. The manufacturing of toys in America is a major industry, comparable to that of automobiles and cosmetics; children pass quickly from "The Farmer in the Dell" to the latest dance craze, from tag to organized Little League; hundreds of riding vehicles have replaced the homemade wagon, and "Tom Walkers" are made of steel and plastic, not tin cans, string, and discarded lumber; but jacks, marbles, and jump ropes are still the best buy for your money, and thousands of counting-out and jump-rope rhymes are chanted every day.

So many informants, ranging from third graders to octogenarians, reported these Alabama folk games that we finally decided on composite reportings that include variant rules, skills, and methods. Readers will probably remember many other ways of playing them. Unfortunately, we were obliged to sacrifice the language of the informants for the sake of clarity.

Hide-and-Go-Seek

The seeker or "it" (and children usually start the game off by chanting "Not I it! Not I it!," until "it" is chosen by common assent or a counting-out rhyme) hides his eyes, amid shouts of "you're peeking!" and counts, usually to fifty or a hundred, while the others hide—and there's the real fun. Younger children will hide in obvious places or with older ones. Often a daring player will search out another hiding place in the middle of the game. For the hider, the object is to reach base—a designated tree, rock, or wall of the house—thereby avoiding being named "it" for the next game. He may either wait in his hiding place until he is discovered and try to outrun the seeker, or he may slip from his place and soundlessly, slyly reach home or base. The seeker must not only seek but also give chase, often to several players simultaneously, for his object is to tag somebody for "it" in the next game. After he has finished counting, the seeker cries out:

> Bushel of wheat, bushel of rye,
> Who's not ready, holler I. (or holler out)

Sometimes, somebody will. Then the seeker will cry:

> Bushel of wheat, bushel of clover,
> Who's not hid, can't hide over.
> Ready or not, here I come!

That is the signal that the game is beginning in earnest. When the seeker captures a player, he calls out to the others who are still hidden:

> Ole, Ole, Olsen, All in free!

or simply:

> All in free!

And the game begins anew. Hide-and-Go-Seek is usually played in fine weather, just at dusk or in first dark, the time of the game an added excitement, though it is also played in broad daylight. An enduring game of immemorial date, it is a fine frolic loved even by older children. There are precious few Alabamians who cannot remember the excitement of "Ready or not, here I come!" and there are a good many of us who still carry the scar of a nail or a piece of broken glass we stepped on as we ran around the fig tree, under the barbed-wire fence, through gap to base, home free.

[*Note:* Lomax collected several hide-and-seek chants from Sumter County, Alabama, in 1937, 1939, and 1940, during his research for the Library of Congress.]

Here We Go Round the Mulberry Bush

A circling game in which children pantomime various actions as they sing, "Here We Go Round the Mulberry Bush" is extremely popular with the grades 1–3.

> Here we go round the mulberry bush,

the mulberry bush, the mulberry bush,
Here we go round the mulberry bush,
On a cold and frosty morning
(or, So early in the morning).

This is the way we wash our hands,
Wash our hands, wash our hands,
This is the way we wash our hands,
On a cold and frosty morning.

The stanzas continue indefinitely with the way we: wash clothes, mend clothes, sweep the floor, etc. Usually there is a leader who calls out the desired pantomime, frequently the teacher. The chant is derived from Mother Goose.

The Farmer in the Dell

A circling-singing game in which one player in the center of the ring, the farmer, chooses a wife who joins him and, on the next stanza, chooses a child. The choosing continues until the end of the song, as the circle grows smaller and smaller. The song itself belongs to the same category as "The Old Woman and Her Pig," "The House that Jack Built," and "This Is the Key of the Kingdom." The dependent relationship that such poems establish are a delight to children.

The farmer's in the Dell, the farmer's in the Dell,
Heigh-o the derry-o, the farmer's in the Dell.
The farmer takes a wife, the farmer takes a wife,
Heigh-o the derry-o, the farmer takes a wife.

The wife takes the child

. . . .

The child takes the nurse

. . . .

The nurse takes the dog

. . . .

The dog takes the cat

. . . .

The cat takes the rat

. . . .

The rat takes the cheese

. . . .

The cheese stands alone.

We're Sailing Round the Ocean
(We're Marching Round the Levee)

"We're Sailing Round the Ocean" is a circling game accompanied by song and pantomime. There are two basic variations. In the first, a boy and a girl are chosen to stand in the center of the circle; they pantomime the actions mentioned in the song while the other children link hands and circle. In the other, all the children participate in the pantomime—slightly more complicated and a good bit more democratic. The players pair off in couples, boy and a girl, boy and a girl, much as in square dancing. In the first stanza, which is also the chorus and is often sung between each stanza, though just as often sung only at the beginning and end of the game, the children link hands and circle in time with the song, a lively but sweet tune with a kind of

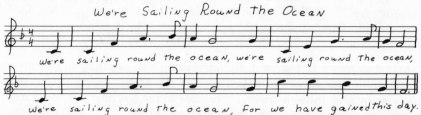

skipping rhythm. On subsequent stanzas they cease circling, stand in place, and partners pantomime the action: turn to face the sweetheart, join hands, stretch out arms to show how much they love, and then kneel, all of these accompanied by giggles and blushes. They curtsy, bow and bid farewell, drop hands, and "Go in and out your window"; the dancers again circle, this time in a sort of do-see-do, going around each other until they return to their original partners or until they tire of going in and out. Finally, they repeat the chorus, linking hands and circling.

We're sailing round the ocean,   Go forth and face (meet) your lover,
We're sailing round the ocean,   Go forth and face your lover,
We're sailing round the ocean,   Go forth and face your lover,
For we have gained this day,   For we have gained this day.
(As we have gone before).

    I take his hand and greet him (you)

    I measure my love to show him (you)

    I kneel because I love him (you)

    Good-bye, I hate to leave you.

    Go in and out your window.

    We're sailing round the ocean.

[*Note:* Richard Chase, in *American Folk Songs and Tales* (New York: New American Library of World Literature, 1962), describes this ring game as largely pantomimic with a couple, a boy and a girl, in the center ring while the others circle, remain in position, or drop hands. The familiar Alabama version is more like a square dance. Chase reports several other stanzas, similar to "Here We Go Round the Mulberry Bush": Go fasten down the shutters, Go jumping over the doorsills, Go wash your tiny windows, Go up and down the ladders. He says that when nearly all the players are inside the ring, the children circle in scattered groups, and the last round ends with couples swinging each other.]

Jackstones

Any number of players, ordinarily one to five girls. The first player scatters jacks and picks up "ones"—that is, she throws the ball into the air, retrieves the jacks one by one and catches the ball, after it bounces once, with the same hand. The retrieved jack is placed in the other hand. If she picks up all the scattered "ones" without dropping ball and jack and without her fingers touching any other jack, then she proceeds to twos, threes, fours, and so on. (This is not always easy; often it requires the deftest touch, for if the nearest jack so much as moves, the player misses.) If and when she misses, the turn passes to the next player. When her turn comes again, she will pick up on

whatever number she missed. A skilled player will often progress all the way to the end without missing. The last numbers to pick up—say the twelves, thirteens, and fourteens—are most difficult: they require a short scatter and a long scooping motion for recovery. Sometimes, players will require "tricks." Two popular tricks are "pigs in the poke" and, after the game is won, "pigs over the stile." In "pigs in the poke," the left hand rests on the playing surface in a cupped position, thumb loosely held along fingers. Jacks are recovered and thrown into the cup or "poke" while the ball is either in air or bouncing. "Pigs over the stile" requires the player to retrieve the jack and make a hopping motion over the cupped hand—the jack must touch the playing surface on both sides of the stile. Many times there are jacks play-offs, where tricks are extremely important. In some play-offs, right-handed players will switch to the left hand, left-handed players to the right.

The playing pieces are 6 to 12 or more (a skilled player can use up to 30) six-pronged pieces and a rubber ball. The game is universal and of prehistoric age; the playing pieces may be knucklebones of small animals, smooth pebbles, or seeds. Thirty years ago in the United States, it was still often played with small rocks, without a ball. The object, whether or not there is a ball, is to release the jacks, either by scattering or throwing into the air, and then to capture as many as possible. The older, more primitive form of the game—tossing the jacks into the air and retrieving them on the back of the hand—is now used either as a way of determining who shall scatter first, or as a way of ascertaining whether the player starts on his "twos," "threes," etc. Some players can catch ten or so jacks on the back of the hand—the fingers must be rigid, pointed up to form a shallow resting place for the jacks.

Leapfrog

Five to twenty or more players form a line, body space between each player. The last player in line "leaps" over each of the others, who are on all fours, head down, rump high, until he reaches the end of the line, whereupon he assumes the frog position. This process continues until all the players have leaped over the "frogs."

It is not surprising that one of the physical feats necessary for man's survival became a game, a sport, and, in ballet, an art form. There are numerous pictorial references to leaping as a game in early civilizations—leaping the bull was, judging from statuary and painted vases and friezes, a national sport in ancient Crete. The American folk game of leapfrog is primarily a frontier, rough-and-tumble sport for boys, though very young girls sometimes play it. It requires little dexterity, especially in small children who sort of roll over the "frog," and provokes much merriment.

I Spy, I Love My Love With An A

These are guessing games. "I Love My Love With An A" is alphabetic. The speakers utter the formula, the others guess (an apple, an arrow). "I Spy" is more general. The player may spy something red, round, as well as something that begins with a particular letter. In both games, the object is supposed to be in view of all the players.

[*Note:* A more complicated version of these games, enjoyed by both adults and children, is "My Ship Comes in Loaded With" in which players name an object for each letter of the alphabet, repeating the previously named objects. For example, the player whose turn is *f* must not only name, say, *f*ish, but also *a*pples, *b*ananas, *c*ats, *d*ogs, and *e*ggs. Hence, "My Ship" is primarily a game of memory skills based on verbal and imagistic associations. If the players are word lovers, the game can take on keen intellectual excitement.]

Blindman's Buff

One player is designated the blindman. He is blindfolded and spun around three times. He must locate another player and correctly identify him—not an easy task when thirty players are scattered over a playground. Only then can the blindfold be removed. The player who is caught and identified becomes the next blindman. Teachers keep watch to prevent accidents.

London Bridge

Two players link hands, lift arms above shoulders to form an arch. They secretly designate themselves as chocolate or vanilla. The other children pass through the arch as everybody sings "London Bridge." When a player is passing through the arch he may be captured; that is, the arch falls on him. He is asked in a whisper, "Which do you want, chocolate or vanilla?" (or lemon or orange etc.). When he chooses, he lines up behind whichever member of the arch he had named. This process is repeated until all players have lined up behind "chocolate or vanilla." Then a line is drawn in the dirt. The teams pull against each other until one succeeds in drawing the other over the line.

London Bridge is falling down,
Falling down, falling down.
London Bridge is falling down,
My fair lady.

Build it up with gold and silver,
Gold and silver will not stay (rust away)
Build it up with iron bars,
Iron bars will bend and break.

The above stanzas are sung as the children pass under the arch.

London Bridge is falling down,
Falling down, falling down.
London Bridge is falling down,
And it shall fall on you.

Arch falls, a player is captured, and the children sing:

Here's a prisoner I have got.

Arch takes prisoner aside, asks him to choose sides, and leads him back
to place him behind his leader, singing:

Take the key and lock him up.

The chants are repeated until all the children have chosen sides.
Additional stanzas are often added.

Telling Fortunes

One child counts out another's buttons, saying:

> Rich man, poor man,
> Beggar man, thief,
> Doctor, lawyer,
> Merchant, chief.

Whatever term the last button comes out on determines the profession of the man she will marry. Or, they might say:

> Tinker, tailor,
> Soldier, sailor.

Pease Porridge Hot

A hand-clapping game played in various ways. Two children clap against each other and with their own hands saying,

> Pease Porridge Hot,
> Pease Porridge Cold,
> Some like 'em (it) hot,
> Some like 'em cold,
> Some like 'em
> In the pot,
> Nine days old.

Some scholars think that *pease* in "Pease Porridge Hot" refers to a porridge made of legumes (which were also ground up for pease flour and pease meal, hence pease-bread and pease-loaf); others interpret pease in the sense of *peace*, hence a porridge made to quiet a fretful baby. The *Oxford English Dictionary* cites a reference from Caxton in which pease are so hot they burn the hand, indicating a pepper, and that meaning would seem to be supported by the association of pease with *hot pease* in children's jump-rope rhymes. For centuries, *pease* was both singular and plural, *pea* gradually evolving as the singular and *peas* and *pease* as the plural. Both *pea* and *pease* were reported by our informants; the variant spellings may be explained, then, according to the specific informant, some holding on to the older form, others taking up the new.

In the past decade or so the "Mary (or Merry) Mack" clapping game has replaced "Pease Porridge Hot," which exists now primarily as a nursery rhyme. Our own children play "Mary Mack," often with progressive intensity and speed—slow and light to hard and fast. (See jump-rope rhymes for text of "Mary Mack.") Nonverbal clapping games are also current among junior high school students—these are distinguished by quite complicated and often rapid rhythmical patterns, involving both hand and thigh. The hand-clapping itself offers fine possibilities for investigators in folklore, music, and dance, but it has been largely ignored. Still prominent in primitive societies, clapping is often accompanied by a chant. It may be a bit odd to conceive of the hand as a musical instrument, but it is precisely that, functioning much like percussion, the bass viol, and various bass horns, which provide either the beat or a fugal counterpoint. As accompaniment to both music and the spoken chant, its use is universal. Why clapping became a symbol of approbation is unknown—but mass clapping is a stylized, symbolic gesture of approval. Clapping became an element of audience participation and approval in coffee-house and street-protest folk songs in the 1950s, and its use in Negro hymn singing is well documented. The gesture itself is, initially, a spontaneous expression of joy, easily observable in children, and the psalmist of the Old Testament refers to the clapping of hands in joy before the Lord. The most interesting and widespread use of hand clapping lies now in school cheers, another segment of contemporary folk survivals and adaptations neglected by folklore scholars. The cheers themselves reflect usage of the versified taunt and riddle, the folk holler, and the chant.

Froggie-in-the-Millpond

Any number of players link hands and circle around the "frog" in the center of the ring while they chant:

> Froggie in the millpond,
> Can't get out, Can't get out.
> Froggie in the millpond,
> Can't get out,
> Take a little stick
> And stir him out.

Players close their eyes to allow frog to hide, then yell "Where's the frog?" as they search. Whoever finds him becomes the new frog. The "stinkpot" variation in "Drop-the-Handkerchief" is derived from "Froggie-in-the-Millpond," and children still torment frogs by poking them with sticks to make them jump. Compare the game song here with the "Froggie" rhyme that appears in the section on Taunts; note how the song expands and elaborates the oral chant. This kind of transfer occurs often in folk rhyme.

Tag

One player is chosen *it*; he pursues the other children until at last he tags one who subsequently becomes *it*. Usually there is a "base," a tree or rock, which a player may reach and thereby claim immunity from the pursuer—"I'm on base!" or simply "Base!" Often the children who are eluding the chaser sing:

> Ain't no buggers out tonight,
> Out tonight,
> Ain't no buggers out tonight,
> Daddy killed them all last night.

Ring-around-the-Rosy

The oldest and best known of all circling-singing folk games, "Ring-around-the-Rosy," is played with any number of children. The players link hands and circle, chanting "Ring-around-the-Rosy, Ring-around-the-Rosy, A pocket full of posies," as many times as they like until someone, not necessarily the leader although it is usually he, cries out "Guinea, Guinea all squat!" Players immediately squat or sit, still holding hands (unless they are very young, in which case, there is a good bit of tumbling, falling, and general merriment); the last to squat is out of the game. The chanting and circling resume until by the process of elimination a winner is declared. Often, the player who is last to squat in any sequence rejoins the game after he has paid a forfeit—usually telling a sweetheart's name. The song itself is quite old, but was not, according to the Baring-Goulds in their work *The Annotated Mother Goose*, printed until 1881, in Kate Greenaway's *Mother Goose*. A simplified version of "Ring-around-the Rosy" is "Big Guinea, Little Guinea" in which players form a ring and chant in unison "Big guinea, little guinea, all squat." The last to squat is eliminated. The act and chant are repeated until only one is left standing.

Little Sally Walker (Waters)

Little (or Miss) Sally Walker sits in the center of a ring weeping while the others circle around her, singing. There are many versions of the folk tune they sing, but the one most common in Alabama seems to be:

Little Sally Walker, sitting in a saucer,
Crying and weeping for what she has done,
Rise, Sally, rise, wipe your weeping eyes,
Put your hand on your hip,
Shake it to the East, shake it to the West,
Shake it to the one you like the best.

Each player takes a turn as Sally Walker and performs the implied actions. Often the other players add steps of their own or perform the same actions as Sally Walker. *The Annotated Mother Goose* reports that the song first appears in 1886, *Mother Goose's Nursery Rhymes,* as a song for the game "Kiss in the Ring."

Sally, Sally Waters, sprinkle in the pen,
Nie, Sally! Hie, Sally, for a young man!
Choose for the best,
Choose for the worst,
Choose for the prettiest that you like best.

Drop-the-Handkerchief

Players form a circle, leaving space between each child. One player, *it*, stands in the center of the ring with a handkerchief in his hand. He then circles the outside of the ring and surreptitiously drops the handkerchief behind any player he chooses. The second player must pick up the handkerchief and give chase. If the first player or *it* is overtaken, he must be the "dropper" again in a second round. Otherwise, he runs to the space vacated by his pursuer, who then becomes the dropper or odd-man-out. Sometimes, the captured runner will also be forced to pay the forfeit of telling his sweetheart's name. Or he may be placed in the center of the ring, "the stinkpot," as the children shout, "Johnny's in the stinkpot, Can't get out, Can't get out!" while the dropper continues to circle the ring and drop the handkerchief behind another player. Meanwhile, the child in the stinkpot, who has the advantage of seeing where the handkerchief falls, can steal it, get out of the stinkpot, and pursue the dropper. The stinkpot represents a complication of the original game of tag. The children will often chant:

> I lost my handkerchief yesterday,
> Just found it today, and it was full of mud,
> And I throwed it away.

or

> A tisket, A tasket
> A green and yellow basket,
> Wrote a letter to my fellow,
> And on the way,
> I dropped it, I dropped it.

Bum, Bum, Bum, Here We Come

This game is played between two groups of children. The object of the game is for one group to guess what the other group is making or doing. In the game one group runs toward the other and says:

> Group 1—Bum, bum, bum
>   Here we come.

> Group 2—Where are you from?

> Group 1—New York (or Chicago, Detroit, etc.)

> Group 2—What's your trade?

> Group 1—Sweet lemonade.

> Group 2—Well, get to work and get it made.

Group 1 begins to pantomime what they are making, and Group 2 guesses. The turn passes to Group 2 unless they do not answer correctly. In such case, Group 1 takes another turn.

Red Rover, Red Rover

Children choose sides, form two opposing lines several yards apart, and link hands. Side A yells, "Red Rover, Red Rover, send Johnny right over." The chosen child runs towards the enemy. If he breaks through the line, he chooses a captive and returns to his home side. If he fails, he himself becomes a captive. The turn passes to Side B, the action is repeated, each side taking turns, until one side captures all the players of the opposing team—or until the bell rings. The winning team is the one with the most captives. Red Rover is a strenuous game that sometimes results in injuries; it is not popular with teachers and is often forbidden.

Molly, Molly Bright

Draw two lines on the ground about thirty feet apart. Draw one line halfway between. Even numbers of players on each side stand on home lines. One group advances to center line; the leader on opposing sides says, "Molly, Molly Bright." The advanced group says, "How far is it to granny's house?" The other side says, "Three score and ten." First team, "Can we get there by candlelight!" Other team says, "Yes, if your legs are long and light." First team turns and runs for home, and the other team tries to catch them before they get to the line. If any are caught, they must join the other team. Then, the other side advances and goes through the same routine; the team that captures all their enemies wins. The dialogue of this game perhaps derives from the nursery rhyme "How Many Miles to Babylon," itself a rhyme for an English game "Barley Bridge," similar to "London Bridge."

Fox and Hound

As many people as want to can play this game, but there must be an equal number of boys and girls. The boys are called "hounds" and the girls "foxes." A home base must be established. The hounds stay at the home base and give the foxes a three-minute hiding period. After the three-minute period the hounds go out looking for the foxes. When a hound finds a fox, he must take her back to home base; when everyone has returned to home base, the hound and the fox he captured remain "sweethearts" the rest of the evening.

Fox and Hound (another version)

This game is played mostly by boys. One side is referred to as "hounds" and the other "foxes." The hounds give the foxes a five-minute start and then begin hunting them. All the foxes must be caught before the game is over. When all the foxes have been captured and returned to home base, the teams swap sides.

Stealing Sticks

As many as want to can play this game. One team stays on one side and
a second team on the other side of a center line. Each team draws a
circle in one corner of the back area and places twelve sticks in the
circle. The object of the game is for one of the teams to get the other
team's sticks one at a time without getting caught. If a player gets
caught, he is placed in the "hole," which is a circle near the sticks. If
someone is in the "hole," one of his team members can tag him and free
him instead of getting a stick. The game continues until one team gets
all the other's sticks, or all the members of one team are in the "hole."

Hounds and Deer

One boy takes a pocketful of paper torn into bits and goes off into the
woods. He is supposed to drop a bit of paper at intervals of about ten
counts as scent for the hounds. His object is to elude the hounds and
travel to a designated spot and back without the hounds catching him.
All the other boys are hounds, and they must follow the scent. Sometimes as many as three boys act as dogs, and the others are the
huntsmen. "Hounds and Deer" is a variation of "Fox and Geese."
Another similar capture game is "Prison Base," where two sides attempt to take prisoners across a line of division.

Crack the Whip

Any number of players line up and hold hands. The leader, usually a
strong fellow, starts running in a straight line, drawing the line of
players behind him. Suddenly he swerves to one side and pulls with all
his might; the players near the bottom of the line are thrown tumbling
and rolling with great force.

Sling the Statues

The "slinger" slings each player and releases him. The player freezes in
the position in which he falls, and must remain a statue until all the
players have been slung. If he cannot maintain the position, he is out of
the game. The last one standing becomes the next "slinger" or is
declared the winner. This game allows for a good bit of cheating—a
player can easily alter his position when the slinger isn't looking, but
invariably the other children catch him and call for his dismissal from

the game. The oddity of the statues' positions is one of the most enjoyable aspects of "Sling the Statues."

Rock School

One child is chosen teacher, by common assent or a counting-out rhyme. The other children sit on the top step. The "teacher" comes to each player with crossed fists, and the player must guess which fist holds the rock in order to progress to the next step or "grade." The player who reaches the bottom step first becomes the teacher in the next game. "Rock School" is a slow game played mostly by girls—its slowness permits a good deal of visiting, chatting, and laughter. Frequently, teacher reprimands pupils for not paying attention.

Mother, May I?

The leader or "mother" stands a good distance from any number of players. To each player she issues commands: "Suzy, take three giant steps," or baby steps, regular steps, any number or kind the mother chooses, usually one to three. If the player advances without asking, "Mother, May I?" or is not given permission (almost always granted) "Yes, you may," he must revert to his original position. The first player to reach Mother becomes leader in the next game. "Mother, May I?" is a variation of Simon Says, wherein the leader, "Simon," issues various commands: "Simon Says, touch your toes," "Simon Says, sit down," and the players obey. If the command is not prefaced by the phrase "Simon Says," the player must not perform the command. If he does, he is out of the game. These games are played indoors on rainy days as well as on the playground.

Hopscotch

Hopscotch is a progressive hopping game played with any number of children. Each child has a toy, either a bit of glass or a rock, the playing piece which he must throw accurately into the appropriate blocks ("scotches") of the playing area, marked on the dirt with a sharp stick or chalked on a sidewalk.

The first player tosses his toy into block 1, hops on one foot from blocks 1 through 9, where he turns around, still on one foot, returns to block 1, retrieves his toy, and tosses for block 2. He progresses in like manner until he misses, either by landing his toy on the line or outside the playing area, or by failing to hop, thus relinquishing his turn to the next player. The player may miss in any block, or he may advance until he has thrown his toy into the last block, hopped to retrieve his toy, and returned to the starting point. The first player to accomplish this feat is the winner, although some purists require (or the players agree) that the game be played again in reverse, that is, with block 9 as the starting point.

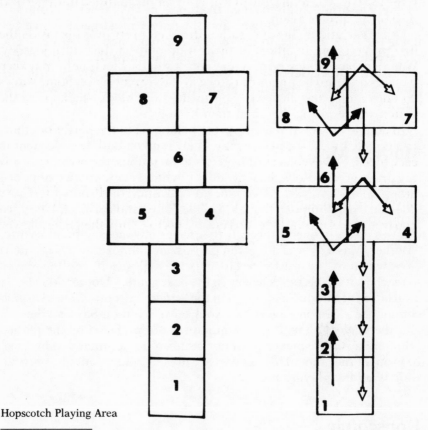

Hopscotch Playing Area

[*Note:* Sometimes, blocks 2 and 3 are omitted or placed after the doubles, block 4 and 5. Additional blocks are often added to block 9, usually two.]

Some collectors report that children chant a nursery rhyme as they play hopscotch:

Two little birdies sitting on a limb,
One named Jack, one named Jim.
Fly away Jack, Fly away Jim.
Come back, Jack, Come back Jim.

Many children introduce a complication. No player is allowed to touch a block in which another player's toy lies. Hence, if your toy lands in block 3, you must hop over blocks 1 and 2, if they contain other toys. You must land your toy in the natural progression; thus it may fall in a block that already contains a toy. To retrieve the toy on the return trip, a player must stand on one foot in the block nearest the disputed block and reach for it, not hop into it, as he ordinarily would. If the toy lands on a line, the player is either disqualified until the next turn or he throws again.

Other variations: In some games the player retrieves his toy on the first progression; in others he picks it up only on the return journey. When a player misses, he may leave his toy in the block, or he may keep it on his honor to begin his next turn at the correct place. Some games do not require the player to hop to the final block—he hops to the scotch where his toy lies, and then he hops out.

In double blocks: If there is no toy belonging to the player or others in a double block, the player may safely land on both feet, one foot in each block; however, according to some variations, the presence of any toy in a given block has no effect whatsoever on the hopper's progression—in these games, the complication of disputed territory does not exist. Suppose, though, a player's toy lands in block 4: he must hop from 3 to 4 on one foot and retrieve his toy. Only then is he allowed to put the other foot in block 5.

A few contributors played hopscotch using an area shaped like a snail shell. The toy is tossed into a square. The player jumps over the

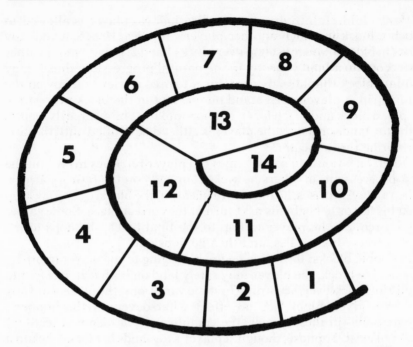

square containing his toy and proceeds to the center where he turns around, never allowing both feet to touch the ground, jumps out square by square until he is next to the square containing his toy. He then picks up his toy and hops out, square by square. He may advance until he misses—either his toy fails to land, clear of lines, in the assigned square, or he touches both feet on the ground simultaneously.

Here We Go Loop-dy Loo

In this circle singing game the players do not move to the left or right, but to the center. With linked hands they surge to the center on "Here we go loop-dy loo," retreat to the larger outside circle on "Here we go loop-dy li," come together at the center again on "Here we go loop-dy loo," retreat on "All on a Saturday night." In the next stanza players maintain the circle, put the right foot forward and tap it in time to the song, shake the foot three times and make a full turn. The actions of the loop-dy-loo chorus are repeated between each stanza. Subsequently, similar actions are performed for the left foot, right hand, and left hand. Then the dancers jump into the circle, shake "the whole self" three times, and turn around. The game ends with another repetition of the chorus. A modern derivation of this game is the Hokey-Pokey, a children's dance that adds more complicated steps to the shaking, turning, and circling.

Chorus
Here we go loop-dy loo,_
Here we go loop-dy lī (lee, la),
Here we go loop-dy loo,
All on a Saturday night.

I put my right foot in,
I take my right foot out,
I give my foot a shake, shake, shake,
And turn myself about.

Chorus

Here we go loop-dy loo, etc.

(I put my left foot in)

Chorus
(I put my right hand in)

Chorus
(I put my left hand in)

Chorus
(I put my whole self in)

Chorus

Stiff Starch

Two children, usually girls, hold hands very tightly, one with palms
up, the other with palms down, the fingers held rigid at the first joint.
On tiptoe, they whirl around and around, their bodies as stiff as
possible, until one or both collapse.

Fruit-Basket-Turn-Over

Usually played inside on rainy days or at parties, "Fruit-Basket-Turn-Over" resembles musical chairs without music. The leader or *it* whispers the name of a fruit to every seated player. (Usually the seating arrangement is circular.) Then he calls, "Apples and pears change places." The children so named follow the command. In the ensuing scramble, *it* tries to get a chair. He continues until he succeeds, and whoever is without a chair becomes the next caller. The leader may call, "Fruit basket, turn over!," in which case all the players seek another chair. That, of course, is the biggest scramble of all.

Club Fist

All players make fists and stack them on each others' in random order. Then one, the chosen leader, asks, "What you got there?" to the player whose fist rests on top. Answer: "Club fist." Question: "What do you want done with it—take it off, blow it off, pinch it off, or crow it off?" The player answers which one he wants, the leader obliges with the requisite action, and the procedure is repeated through the last fist. Our informants do not specify, but "crow it off" probably refers to a "peck," such as the one administered in "Feed the Crow." The fist is often an element in folk play, perhaps a childish reflection of the very real manly fist of free-for-all's and single combat. In the counting-out rhyme "One Potato," the fist is preferred to an extended hand—the leader makes a fist and taps the fists of the players as he chants. In a rather lawless, nonverbal counting-out ceremony, players pile fist over fist or hand over hand and, at a given or understood signal, players shift positions, hand on the bottom progresses to the top. At first the gestures are orderly enough, but as the shifting continues there is a wild scramble to be on top and, hence, be first at whatever game is being played.

Another variation on "Club Fist" is an action game for two or more players, usually found among boys in the upper elementary grades who play the game while the girls are playing jacks. The game is very popular when bad weather prevents playing more active, outdoor games. The object of the game is to inflict enough physical discomfort to cause players to drop out. The one who stays with the game after all others have dropped out wins. If time for play runs out or there is an evident stalemate, those with the reddest skin are declared losers. However, as with most children's games, the playing is the important thing.

There is usual and general acceptance of four basic symbols for use in the game: the clenched fist represents "rock"; the extended index finger, "dynamite"; the clenched fist with extended and open middle and index fingers, "scissors"; and the open hand extended palm down and horizontally, "paper." It is also agreed that "rock" can crush "scissors," but "dynamite" can blow up "rock," and "paper" can cover it up; "paper" can cover up "dynamite" and "rock," but "scissors" can cut "paper"; "dynamite" can blow up "rock" and "paper," but "scissors" can cut it (the fuse?). Some players allow "paper" to cover up "dynamite." The relationship between "paper" and "dynamite" must be decided before play begins. Finally, "scissors" can cut "dynamite" and "paper," but "rock" can crush it.

All players form fists with their right hands and in unison stamp their left palms with their fists. On the third stroke each player forms one of the four symbols. Any players whose symbol has power over another may strike the player who has made the less powerful symbol on the underside of his wrist with the index and middle fingers of his right hand. For example, if three players form "scissors," "rock," and "dynamite," the player who made "scissors" may strike the player who formed "dynamite," since "scissors" can cut "dynamite." The player who formed "rock" may strike the player who formed "scissors," because "rock" can crush "scissors." Also, the player who formed "dynamite" can strike the player who formed "rock," since "dynamite" can blow up "rock."

Show Your Teeth

Another folk game that involves physical punishment is a lengthy dialogue of the dependency nursery rhyme variety. One informant offered only the dialogue, but others remembered playing the game in grade school. Players may sit or stand, usually in a semicircle. A leader-interrogator is chosen. He goes about to players asking the various questions; they supply the appropriate responses—one question to one player. Anyone who "shows" his teeth, that is, grins or laughs, is punished as the rhyme indicates. Punishment is usually a symbolic gesture, but it may be quite real. Implicit in this game, as in "Club Fist," is the element of cruelty. "Rotten Egg" is a similar game, minus the dialogue. In the schoolroom or any gathering where certain rules of decorum prevail, children often get the giggles. Somebody will holler, "First one that laughs is a rotten egg!" For a few moments, all is quiet. Finally, one smiles, another "makes faces," and the giggles start all over again.

What you got there?
Bread and cheese.

Where is my share?
Cat got it.
Where is the cat?
In the woods.
Where is the woods?
Fire burnt it.
Where is the fire?
Water squinched it.
Where is the water?
Ox drank it.
Where is the ox?
Butcher killed it.
Where is the butcher?
Rope hung him.
Where is the rope?
Knife cut it.
Where is the knife?
Hammer broke it.
Where is the hammer?
Broke in ten thousand pieces hid under
Grandma's doorstep. Anyone who shows his
teeth gets a hair pull, knock on the head,
pinch and a slap.

Red Light

A group of children line up quite a distance from the child who is the
red light. When the red light's back is turned, he is a green light, and
the children can go toward him, but when he turns and faces them he is
a red light. When he turns and yells, "Red light!" everyone must stop.
If the red light sees a player move, he can tell him to go back to the
beginning line. The first child to reach the red light is the next to be the
"red light." "Red Light" is a twentieth-century adaptation of "Mother,
May I?"

Mumble Pig

Mumble Pig is played with pocketknives that have two blades at one
end. The larger blade is fully opened and the smaller blade is opened
halfway. The player takes the knife by the end of handle, allows the end
of handle and point of small blade to rest on floor or wooden board.
(There are usually only two boys in each game.) The knife is jerked

upward and flipped in the air and comes to rest on the ground. If the small blade sticks deep enough to hold itself up, the player has scored 100 points. If the large blade sticks and holds, he has scored 50 points, and if both blades are sticking and holding the knife, the score is 75 points. The loser has to "root a pig out of the ground" with his nose.

I See a Bear

Players line up in a row, slyly placing someone who doesn't know the game at the opposite end to the leader. The leader, first in line, says, "I see a bear," squats down, and points to the next player. Successive players do likewise. The last player has nobody to point to—the others pile on him. Nowadays, "pile on" is played in Alabama without any preliminaries. Children choose another child and pile on. Tricks played on the uninitiated appear throughout world folklore. "I See a Bear" is closely related to a prank played by rural Alabama adolescents—"Snipe Hunting."

A group of youngsters takes an innocent on a "snipe" hunt. They wander here and there in the woods, carefully instructing the victim in the modes of hunt and the peculiarities of the mythical animal, which they often compare to a squirrel or possum. The darkness and the mock seriousness of the participants generates high spirits—courtship and tales of the supernatural invariably accompany the hunt, and the hunt may go on for several hours. Hunters get lost, some on purpose, shout, shush, enact postures of tracking, and, at last, find the "snipe." The victim is told to wait at a particular "stand" with a croker sack while others run the snipe to his trap. Most likely, the stand is a ditch or gulley. A great shout is raised, the mythical beast is running to its doom—another shout, and the pranksters are off, leaving the innocent with an empty bag.

Most victims know instantly they've been duped, but there are records of folks waiting a good while for the snipe. Usually the prank is played on a younger adolescent, twelve or thirteen years old, one ready to join the group we now call teenagers; hence, the snipe hunt becomes a veiled folk initiation into sexuality and courtship. Once in a great while the hunt takes on a vicious cruelty—as when the victim is left alone in darkness for hours. The college folk prank of leaving the pledge brother tied to a tree near a cemetery is, of course, a near equivalent to the rural snipe hunt, and there are documented cases of death as a result of such fraternity rituals. Most snipe hunts end where they begin—in good fellowship. The editor well remembers her own snipe hunt in 1950 in a community called Blackjack, an outpost of Friendship, in Elmore County, Alabama.

Marbles

The game of marbles, played by nearly every boy and many girls until the mid-twentieth century, when it lost a little of its popularity, requires very little—a few inexpensive marbles (including several extra large ones to be used as "shooters"), good eyes, strong hands, a gambling spirit, and a single ellipsoid drawn on the ground for the playing area, plus a straight line several feet away to be used as "toy." Some players feel that toy ought to encircle the playing area; other players simply draw a large circle and place their marbles in the center and shoot from the outer edge. As one contributor said, "To play the game of marbles there has to be a circle."

The first order of business is for each player to place a certain number of marbles on the straight line drawn through the ellipsoid, or in the middle of the large circle.

In order to establish the order of play, each player tosses his shooter at an established goal—sometimes a separate line, sometimes the toy line. The closest one takes first turn; that is, he attempts to knock the marbles out of the ellipsoid or circle; next closest, second; etc. When his turn comes, each player cradles his shooter in his crooked forefinger, folds the other three fingers into his palm, and places his thumb, nail to marble, behind his shooter. He kneels on the ground, then places his hand on the ground in the shooting position, which is palm up with the base knuckles touching the ground. A flip of the thumb propels the marble. If no marble is knocked out of position, the turn passes to the next player. If a marble is knocked out of the ellipsoid, the player takes the marble and shoots again from the place where his shooter rests. The players return to toy only when all of the marbles have been won. Teachers usually require that marbles be given back to the original owners. However, the version of marbles known as "keeps" was ever the more popular.

Green Gravel

"Green Gravel" is a circling, play-party game for girls. One girl is chosen to stand in the center while the others hold hands and circle around her. On the fifth line, the girl in the center symbolically turns her back to the others, and on the last line she drops her head. Probably the game is a survival of an English country dance, or even an ancient rite of mourning and/or fertility. Byron Arnold collects the song in *Folk Songs of Alabama*, but the tune differs from ours, and his informant calls it a line game in which players choose until all have been chosen. Some enterprising soul in Tallassee, Alabama, where this song and game was collected, evidently had a nicely developed spirit of parody, a common occurrence as folk games evolve.

Green gravel, green gravel,
The grass is so green
The maidens so ugly,
They hate to be seen.

Miss Polly, Miss Polly,
Your sweetheart is dead,
He wrote you a letter,
So turn back your head.

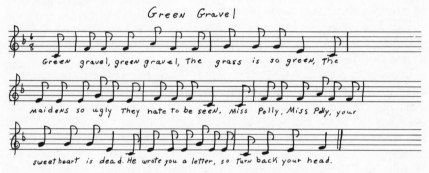

Arnold cites the last two lines of the first stanza:

The prettiest fair maiden
I ever have seen.

Thimble or Button

A popular guessing game, "Thimble or Button" is played at social gatherings by young and old. Players arrange themselves either in a row or semicircle. Any number can play. A leader holds the thimble or button in his hands in such a manner that the object cannot be seen—heels of hands together, fingers touching and extended, so as to form an inverted V. He passes down the line, sliding his hands into the outstretched hands of each player. To only one player does he give the thimble. When he finishes, he says, "Thimble, Thimble, Who's got the thimble?" The first player in line says, "I think so-and-so's got the thimble." If he guesses correctly, the player with the thimble takes the place of the leader; if not, the guess passes to the next player and continues until the thimble holder is discovered, whereupon the first leader calls out "Rise, Thimble, and go to work!" and the game continues as before. One of our informants, Mrs. Lucille Cornett, of

Luverne, Alabama, told us that her parents and brothers and sisters played "Thimble" around the fireplace after supper. A bystander added emphatically that the most fun was bending down close to the pretty girls.

Mumbally Peg

Take a broomstick and cut off about a three- or four-inch piece, one end of which is sharpened to a point. Use the rest of the stick as a bat. Lay the short piece on the ground and hit the pointed end, using a strong, downward stroke, making the short peg fly into the air. As the peg is in the air, the batter gets three swings to hit the peg as far as he can with the stick bat. After the peg has been hit, the batter's opponent gets twenty jumps to reach the peg. If he reaches the peg in twenty jumps or less, he scores and gets a turn at bat. If the jumper does not reach the peg in twenty jumps, the batter gets the point and drives the peg into the ground, and the jumper has to wiggle the peg out with his teeth, or anything except his hands.

A Note on the Games of Adolescents

Some scholars argue that play-party games like "We're Sailing Round the Ocean" are courtship rituals and that they evolved largely as a result of certain religious prohibitions against social dancing. There are, however, certain obvious and socially acceptable courtship and kissing games still played in Alabama, contemporary versions of older games; for example, "This, That, and the Other," a blindman's buff game of kiss, hug, slap. In the days before automobiles provided the requisite privacy for courtship, "walking" games were extremely popular. The walk itself as a means of socializing or "promenade" has a long Anglo-American history. As a necessary mode of getting from place to place, as physical exercise, and as an antidote for tedium or a spur to the imagination and intellect, the walk appears again and again in English and American fiction; it is often an excuse to show off finery! "Spin the Bottle" is one of the oldest walking games; the kissing here, if any, occurs on the walk, not in the presence of others. "Pleased or Displeased" is a bit more complicated. An interrogator goes from player to player, asking "Pleased or Displeased?" The answer is generally "Displeased." The next question is, "What would it take to please you?" The player then designates an action, anything from commanding another player to sing a song or stand on his head to a "walk" or a public hug or kiss. "Pleased or Displeased" is a pleasant, slow game that allows for conversation, fellowship, and merriment.

Another kissing game played by adolescents is "Heavy, Heavy Hangs Over Your Head." The leader holds one hand over the eyes of a player (or blindfolds him); with the other hand he dangles some object—an earring, key, watch—and the following dialogue ensues:

Leader: Heavy, heavy hangs over your head.
Player: Fine or superfine? (That is, does it belong to a boy or a girl?)
Leader: Fine.
Player: What will it take to redeem it?

The leader then specifies kisses, hugs for another given player, and the turn passes to whoever has been kissed. The forfeit need not be a kiss—it may be some ridiculous action.

A leader, it ought to be noted, is generally chosen by acclamation or general understanding on account of his natural gifts—not by counting-out rhymes, as in children's games. A descendant of the Master of Revels, he is not only a born leader, but a wit, a master performer, and an astute psychologist of human behavior who establishes and guides relationships within the group. And, often, he or she has not the joyful encumbrance of the followers—a sweetheart. For example, in the adolescent game "Laugh and Go Foot," the leader is directly responsible for the laughter and the game itself—he appears before the players who either stand or sit in a line, and his antics must produce the desired laughter and the exit to the "foot" of the line. Here, the leader is seen clearly in his role as Fool or Master of Revels.

A variant of "Laugh and Go Foot" is "Kitty-Wants-a-Corner," played by both children and adolescents. The odd-man-out, or "poor Kitty," wanders from chair to chair, meowing piteously and chanting "Kitty-wants-a-corner." Players may stroke his head and murmur "poor Kitty." The first to laugh must surrender his chair to the wanderer and take his turn as Kitty.

In "Cross Questions and Crooked Answers," the leader assigns to each player a set answer; then he "goes down the line" putting a question to the participants, who must reply with the previously designated answer or pay a forfeit. The fun, of course, arises from the disparity between questions and answers: illogical relationships, incongruent events and descriptions, absurd juxtapositions, nonsensical images, and ridiculous situations. Here, the leader's primary characteristic is intellectual: he must be quick witted, inventive, and acutely conscious of irony. Sometimes, the leader is an adult, but more often he is another adolescent whom his peers readily identify and select because of his well-known powers of buffoonery, wit, and intelligence.

★☆★☆★☆★☆★☆★☆★☆★☆★☆★☆★☆

Jump-Rope Rhymes

One of the most familiar of all children's games is jump rope. The simplicity with which it fulfills the child's need for physical exercise and its almost infinite number of variations partially account for its popularity. These variations are often expressed by the different rhymes which children chant while jumping. In southeast Alabama the Cinderella rhyme is a widely known favorite, recorded by the contributors to this collection more frequently than any other rhyme:

> Cinderella, dressed in yellow,
> Went to town to mail a letter.
> On the way she met her fellow.
> How many kisses did she get?

The child jumps to the rhythm of the rhyme and continues, counting each jump until a miss. The children actually are more interested in how many times the jumper can jump without missing than the hypothetical number of kisses received by a legendary heroine. In other versions the color of the dress is changed, hence dictating a change in rhyme.

> Cinderella, dressed in pink,
> Washed the dishes in the sink.
> How many dishes did she break?

Again the child jumps until a miss occurs, and the number of successful jumps indicates the number of dishes broken by Cinderella and declares the skill of the jumper. A popular variation reflects the natural interest of the child in the life/death cycle.

> Cinderella, dressed in green,
> Died last night at seven fifteen.
> How many cars and trucks came to her
> funeral?

Another familiar jump-rope rhyme found in southeast Alabama tests the child's skill at performing physical actions while jumping. Such a skill jump is:

> Teddy-bear, Teddy-bear, turn around.
>   (The child turns around while jumping.)

Teddy-bear, Teddy-bear, touch the ground.
  (The child touches the ground while jumping.)

Teddy-bear, Teddy-bear, show your shoe.
  (The child must lift foot to show the shoe
  while continuing the jumps on one foot.)

Teddy-bear, Teddy-bear, skit, skat, skiddoo!
  (The child runs out, avoiding being hit
  by the rope.)

Teddy-bear, Teddy-bear, go upstairs.
  (The child runs back into the jumping area
  and jumps rope, moving toward one of the
  rope swingers.)

Teddy-bear, Teddy-bear, say your prayers.
  (The child clasps hands in prayerful
  position.)

Teddy-bear, Teddy-bear, turn out the light.
  (The child makes a motion as of flipping a
  switch.)

Teddy-bear, Teddy-bear, say good-night.
  (The child droops head, closes eyes, and
  jumps out.)

There are a number of comic or teasing jump rhymes. Many of these do not formally end in a count, although the children usually begin to count as soon as the rhyme is ended. On other occasions children may simply chant through as many rhymes as they can recall before missing a jump. Or, as the two following variants demonstrate, they may add extra syllables here and there:

Teacher, teacher, don't whip me.
Whip that fellow behind that tree.
He stole peaches, I stole none.
Teacher, teacher, ain't that fun?

Teacher, teacher, don't whip me.
Whip that fellow behind the tree.
He stole money, I stole honey.
Teacher, teacher, ain't that funny?

Another common comic jump rhyme that does end in a count is:

Yonder comes teacher with a big, fat stick.
Wonder what I made on arithmetic?
  (Counts 5, 10, 15, etc., until a miss occurs. That number is
  the pretended grade.)

Some rhymes force the jumper to divulge secrets (the name of the jumper's sweetheart); some predict the future on the basis of a fated miss (what kind of house the jumper will live in, number of children, future vocation, length of life); others ridicule the teacher (and one of these is downright bawdy); and a good many reflect life in the twentieth century with references such as Tillie the Toiler, Donald Duck, ice-cream soda, lemonade pop, and bubble gum. The one-room schoolhouse and the hickory stick may be only treasured memories, but marbles, jackstones, drop-the-handkerchief, rock school, and jump rope endure.

Some comments on jump rope as a game are in order. Perhaps its primitive counterpart is swinging on vines! At any rate every civiliza-

tion evolved some sport involving ropes and jumping. As an American and Western European folk game, it has nearly always appealed to girls rather than boys, who abandon it early in elementary school, while girls continue to play it, even today, on into high school. Single jump ropes are still an extremely popular toy item, though unfortunately they are poorly made for jumping. Most are all plastic, much too light, and even those with wooden handles utilize lightweight twine. Single or individual jumping is largely a practice skill—its uses for general physical and athletic training is well attested in the sport of boxing.

As a game, jump rope requires physical abilities that girls in particular possess: nimbleness, endurance, and coordination—or at least they possess those qualities at an earlier age than do boys. Skilled jumpers develop their own styles, and many are unbelievably graceful in the execution of jumps and tricks or stunts. Boys invariably jump with both feet, but girls often jump with first one foot and then the other in a sort of light skipping manner. The object of the game is to jump more times than any other player, though exhibition of other skills is highly desirable. One such skill difficult to learn is "running in"—the player must run in while the rope is in motion and begin to jump immediately. She must accurately gauge the position of the rope—just as it passes the peak of the arc, then run in. Other skills and variations are: "hot pease"—jumping as fast as the throwers can throw; "high water, low water" or jumping higher and higher as the rope is raised; "changing bedroom slippers" or revolving about another jumper; "jumping double," which refers to jumping face to face with another player in the confined space of individual jumping, or the most difficult of all jump skills, jumping while two ropes are in motion simultaneously. Throwers are generally teachers or other adults or older girls, since a long arm is required for a good throw. There are some commercially manufactured ropes for jump-rope games, but the best rope is still a heavy-duty rope sold in hardware and implement stores. Better still is a plow line!

Telling Fortunes

Children jump the rope and ask these questions. Whatever word in the answer they miss on constitutes a prediction.

> What kind of evening gown will you marry in?
> Red, yellow, blue, pink, white. (Repeat if
> necessary until one misses.)

> How old will you be when you marry?
> 11, 12, 13, 14, 15, etc.

How many children will you have?
1, 2, 3, 4, etc.

What kind of house will you live in?
Brick, wood, glass, marble, etc.

What kind of car will you have?
Ford, Chevy, Pontiac, etc.

What kind of ring will you have?
Diamond, wedding ring, birthstone, etc.

Do You Love Me?

A child says the letters of the alphabet on each jump until a miss. Then the child thinks of a boy's (or girl's) name that begins with the letter on which the jumper missed. The child begins jumping again, saying:

_____, _____, do you
love me?

Yes, no, a little bit, maybe so.
(Repeat until a miss.)

Wire Briar

Wire briar, limber lock,
Six geese in a flock,
One flew east,
One flew west,
One flew over the cuckoo's nest.

No More Pencils

No more pencils,
No more books,
No more of teacher's
Cross-eyed looks.

Miss, Miss

Miss, Miss, Little Miss, Miss
When she misses, she misses like
this. (Put foot over the rope,
or stop rope any way.)

Rich Man, Poor Man

Rich man, poor man, beggerman, thief,
doctor, lawyer, priest.
(Say this over and over again until you
miss on one of these and that will be
what you will be.)

Which House?

Bricks, sticks, mud, stone.
(Whatever the rope stops on will be the
type house you will live in.)

High Waters

Chant: The Alabama River goes higher,
         higher, higher, etc. (until the
         jumper falls).

Alternate chant: When it rains, the river gets
                 higher, higher, higher, etc.

[*Note:* The purpose of this jump-rope game is to see how high the
jumper can jump.]

Engine, Engine

Engine, engine, number nine,
Moving down Chicago Line,
How many cars do you have?

[*Note:* The above rhyme is also used for counting out. Everyone
stands in a circle. The leader says the rhyme and points to a different
person in succession for each word. The person pointed out by the last
word *have* names a number and is eliminated. Then the leader counts
up to that number, each person left being a number. When he reaches
the said number, the person he lands on states a number and is
eliminated. This game continues until all but one are eliminated, and
the one left is *it.*]

Dr. Brown

Bluebelle, cockleshells, evy-ivy-over.
Dr. Brown, a very good man,
Teaches children all he can;
First to read, then to write
Evy-ivy—you run out!

Margie

Margie drank some marmalade,
Margie drank some pop,
Margie drank some other things
That made her stomach flop;
Whoops went the marmalade,
Whoops went the pop,
Whoops went the other things
That made her stomach flop.

How Many Miles?

Bluebells, cockshells, evy-wy-o (or evy-ivy-over)
My mommy works,
Daddy cuts the meat,
I'm the little meanie who lives across the street.
How many miles do I go?
(Count until you miss.)

Did You Ever?

Did you ever go a-fishing on a sunny day?
Sitting on a log—the log rolled away!
Put your hands in your pocket,
Your pockets in your pants,
Did you ever see a fish do the hootchy-kootchy dance?

[*Note:* This is also widely known as a nonsense rhyme.]

Spanish Dancer

Spanish dancer do the splits,
Spanish dancer do high kicks;
Spanish dancer do the kangaroo,
Spanish dancer—out skidoo!

Tillie the Toiler sat on a boiler;
The boiler got hot,
Tillie got shot,
How many times did Tillie get shot?
One, two, three, etc.

Buster, Buster, climb the tree,
Buster, Buster, slap your knee;
Buster, Buster, throw a kiss,
Buster, Buster, do not miss.

School's Out

School's out.
School's out.
Teacher let the fools out.
One went East,
One went West,
One went up the teacher's dress.

Teddy Bear

Teddy Bear, Teddy Bear, turn around.
Teddy Bear Teddy Bear, touch the ground.
Teddy Bear, Teddy Bear, tie your shoe.
Teddy Bear, Teddy Bear, go upstairs.
Teddy Bear, Teddy Bear, say goodnight.
Teddy Bear, Teddy Bear, turn off the light.
Teddy Bear, Teddy Bear, sat on a pin,
How many inches did it go in?
One, two, three, etc.

[*Note:* The "Teddy Bear" rhyme in the introduction to jump-rope rhymes is used exclusively for the exhibition of skills, while this one has been adapted for counting jumps, "How many inches" referring to the jumps that follow.]

Butterfly

Butterfly, butterfly, turn around.
Butterfly, butterfly, touch the ground.
Butterfly, butterfly, show your shoe.
Butterfly, butterfly, twenty-three to do.
One,
Two,
Three . . . on to twenty-three or until the jumper misses.

Apples and Oranges

Apples are red, oranges are yellow.
What's the initial of your fellow?
A,
B, etc. . . . until a miss and that becomes the boyfriend's
initial.

Creamery Butter

Apple, peaches, creamery butter,
Here's the name of my true lover.
(Call the letters of the alphabet until there is a miss.)
Ask: "Did your boyfriend kiss you last night?"
Jump rope and repeat: "Yes,
                       No,
                       Little bit,
                       Maybe so."
If the jumper doesn't miss, jump hot peas.

Lemonade Pop

Ice-cream soda, lemonade pop,
Tell me the initial of your sweetheart.
(Call the letters of the alphabet until there is a miss.)

Grace, Grace

Grace, Grace, dressed in lace,
Went upstairs to powder her face.
How many boxes of powder did she use?
One, Two, etc. (until player trips on rope).

Tim, Tim

Tim, Tim, sat on a pin.
How many inches did it go in?
One, two, etc.

Ice-Cream Soda

Ice-cream soda, ginger-ale pop.
Tell me the name of your own sweetheart.
(Jump until you come to your sweetheart's
first initial, stop, then jump until you
come to his second initial, and so on.)

Delaware Punch

Ice-cream soda,
Delaware punch,
Tell me the name of your honeybunch.
A,
B,
C, etc. (When the jumper misses she names a boy whose name
begins with the letter on which she missed, and he takes her
place.)

Antarctic-Equator

Participants spell together slowly
A-N-T-A-R-C-T-I-C
As rope is turned "slow motion"
Then spell
E-Q-U-A-T-O-R
Very fast, as rope is turned fast.

Buster Brown

Buster Brown went to town
With his britches upside down.
Out rolled a nickel;
He bought a pickle.
The pickle was sour;
He bought some flour.
The flour was yellow;
He bought a fellow.
The fellow was mean;
He bought a bean.
The bean was hard;
He bought a card.
And on the card
It said, Red Hot Pepper.

Betty, Betty

Betty, Betty, set the table.
Don't forget the Red Hot Peppers.

Mabel, Mabel

Mabel, Mabel set the table.
Don't forget the salt and pepper.

H-O-T spells hot pease

[*Note:* Red Hot Pepper and salt and pepper refer to throwing the rope faster and harder or Hot Pease (peas), a jump skill often arbitrarily imposed by the throwers on a good jumper.]

Down in the Meadow

Down in the meadow where the green grass grows,
Stood a little girl as pretty as a rose.
Along came a pretty boy and kissed her on the nose.
How many kisses did he give her?
(Jump and count until you miss.)

[*Note:* To add a bit of spice, actual names are often used in lines two and three, such as Suzy and Tommy, Mary and Jim.]

Buckle My Shoe

One, two, buckle my shoe;
Three, four, shut the door;
Five, six, pick up sticks;
Seven, eight, shut the gate;
Nine, ten, begin again.

Here Comes the Teacher

Here comes the teacher with the big fat stick,
Now get ready for arithmetic;
One and one are two, two and two are four;
Now get ready for spelling;
Spell cat c-a-t; spell rat r-a-t;
Now get ready for music.
(Turn very fast, sing "Yankee Doodle," and
then run out.)

W-B-Z

Had a little radio,
Put it in free,
Only station I could get,
Was W-B-Z
(Hot peas until jumper misses.)

Donald Duck

Donald Duck is a one-legged, one-legged, one-legged duck.
Donald Duck is a two-legged, two-legged, two-legged duck.
Donald Duck is a three-legged, three-legged, three-legged duck.
Donald Duck is a four-legged, four-legged, four-legged duck.

Jump Skills

1—Jump once and run out.
2—Jump twice and run out.
3—Jump three times and run out.
4—Jump four times and run out.
5—Jump five times and run out.
6—High waters six times.
7—Low waters seven times.
8—Hop eight times.
9—One foot, one eye closed, nine times.
10—Jump ten times with both eyes closed.
11—Cross feet and jump eleven times.
12—Cross feet and jump twelve times.

[*Note:* This is the most complicated series of jump skills we collected.]

Old Moly Rier

Old Moly Rier jumped in the fire.
The fire was so hot she jumped in the pot.
The pot was so black she jumped in a crack.
The crack was so high she jumped in the sky.
The sky was so blue she jumped in the flue.
The flue was so deep she jumped in the creek.
The creek was so shallow she jumped in the tallow.
Tallow was cold, she jumped on a pole.
Pole was round and she jumped on the ground.
The ground was white and there she spent the night.

Zickary Zan

Oneray, tworay, zickray, a a
Oneray, tworay, zickray, zan,
Halibow, crackabow,
Windbird, swag tail,
Ten bow tan.

Sleeping Beauty

Sleeping Beauty thinks she's cuties.
All she wears is bathing suities.
If she can jump to twenty-four,
She may have her turn once more.

Tiny Tim

I had a little duckling
Named Tiny Tim,   (solo jumper)
Put him in the bathtub,
Teach him how to swim.

Swallowed a bubble,
Called the doctor,
Call for the nurse,
Call the lady with the big fat purse.

In came the doctor,	(add one jumper)
In came the nurse.	(add another jumper)
In came the lady	(add a fourth jumper)
With the big fat purse.	

Out went the doctor,	(one jumper runs out)
Out went the nurse.	(another jumper runs out)
Out went the lady	(another jumper runs out)
With the big fat purse.	

Mary Mack

Mary Mack, dressed in black
Silver gold buttons down her back.
Ask her ma for fifteen cents
To see the elephant jump the fence.
He jumped so high he touched the sky
And won't come back
Until the Fourth of July.

I Love Coffee

I love coffee,
I love tea,
I love (call the person's name)
To come in with me. (Another jumper runs in, and they jump double.)

Elevator

Fudge-Fudge—call the judge.
Mammy has a newborn baby.
    It is not a girl,
    It is not a boy,
It is just a newborn baby.

Wrap it up in tissue paper,
Put it on the elevator.
First floor, miss, second floor,
Miss, third floor, miss, etc.
(Run out on sixth floor.)

How Many Boys?

I love coffee
I love tea
How many boys
Are stuck on me?
(Count until there is a miss.)

Rooms for Rent

Rooms for rent,
Inquire within,
When I move out,
Let (Ann) move in!

[*Note:* This chant is called by the jumper when he has not missed but, for some reason, wishes to stop without a blemish on his record; sometimes chant is called by throwers.]

Four to Go!

One to make ready,
and two to show,
Three to start,
and four to go!

[*Note:* This rhyme is used for preliminary or warm-up jumps not counted in the final total. The warm-up is used when players do not run in. Also used as a chant for foot races.]

All in Together

All in together, girls,
Never mind the weather, boys,
Hark! Hark!

[*Note:* This chant is called by the throwers for several or all jumpers to run in and jump simultaneously.]

I Hear the Teacher

I hear the teacher tapping on the window.
January, February, March (run out on birthday month);
One, two, three, four, five (run out on birthday date);
Monday, Tuesday, Wednesday (run out on day of birth);
One, two, three, four, five (run out on age).

(Long rope jumping: the players run in from side or
front and attempt to keep on skipping during chanting
of above; run out on birthday month, etc.)

Bubble Gum

Bubble gum, bubble gum,
Chew and blow.
Bubble gum, bubble gum,
Scrape your toe.
Bubble gum, bubble gum,
Tastes so sweet,
Get that bubble gum off your feet.
(runs out)

Cinderella

Cinderella, dressed in yellow,
Went downstairs to mail a letter.
On her way she met her fellow.
How many kisses did he give her?
(Jump until you miss.)

Dressed in Green

Cinderella, dressed in green,
Went upstairs to eat ice cream.
How many spoonfuls did she eat?
(Jump until you miss.)

My Little Sister

My little sister, dressed in pink,
Washed the dishes in a sink.
How many dishes did she break?
One, two, three, and on.

Dressed in Black

Cinderella dressed in black,
Went upstairs and sat on a tack.
How many stitches did it take?
(Count till jumper misses.)

Momma, Momma

Momma, Momma, I am sick
Call the doctor quick, quick, quick.
How many pills must I take?
(Count 1, 2, 3, till jumper misses.)

Quick, Quick, Quick

Mother, Mother, I am sick,
Call the doctor, quick, quick, quick.
Give him a shot, he is sick, sick, sick.

Will I Die?

Mother, Mother, I feel sick.
Call the doctor quick, quick, quick.
Doctor, doctor, will I die?
Yes, my dear, but do not cry.
How many carriages will there be?
One, two, three (count till jumper misses).

How Many Years?

Apple, peach, pumpkin pie.
How many years before I die?
One, two, three, etc.

Not Last Night

Not last night, but the night before,
Twenty-four robbers came knocking at my door.
As they ran in, I ran out.
Here's what they left for me to do.

Spanish dancer turn around.
Spanish dancer touch the ground.
Spanish dancer do the split,
Spanish dancer run out.
(Jumper performs act as indicated by rhyme.)

[*Note:* The first stanza of this rhyme is borrowed from a widely
known nonsense poem.]

Policeman, Policeman

Policeman, policeman, do your duty.
There's a girl in town,
She's an American beauty.
She can wibble
She can wobble
She can do the twist,
But I bet ten dollars
She can't do this!
(Give jumper hot peas.)

The Thread Was Thin

I went down town and met Miss Brown,
She gave me a nickel, I bought a pickle,
The pickle was sour, I bought a flower,
The flower was red, I bought a thread,
The thread was thin, I bought a pin,
The pin was sharp, I bought a harp,
and on this harp I played:

Teddy bear, teddy bear, turn around.
Teddy bear, teddy bear, touch the ground.
Teddy bear, teddy bear, show your shoe.
Teddy bear, teddy bear, now skiddoo!

[*Note:* Another example of a nonsense rhyme wed to a skill-jump chant.]

Alligator Purse

Mother, Mother, I am ill,
Send for the doctor to give me a pill.
In came the doctor,
In came the nurse,
In came the lady with the alligator purse.

Don't Blame Me

Policeman, Policeman, don't blame me,
Blame that boy behind the tree.
He stole sugar, he stole tea.
Policeman, Policeman, don't blame me.

Three Dwarfs

Behind the mountain,
(One, two, three)
Three dwarfs were sitting
(One, two, three).
They didn't drink, they didn't eat,
Just sat there chatting
(One, two, three).

Ipsey, Pipsey

Ipsey, Pipsey, tell me true
Who shall I be married to?
A, B, C, etc.

Dancing Dolly

Dancing Dolly has no sense.
She bought some eggs for fifty-nine cents.
The eggs went bad, Dolly went mad
One, two, three, etc.

K-i-s-s-i-n-g

John and Karen sitting in a tree
K-i-s-s-i-n-g.
First comes love, then comes marriage.
Then comes Karen with a baby carriage.
How many babies did she have?

Dressed in Brown

Cinderella dressed in brown,
Went upstairs to make a gown.
How many stitches did she use?

Powder Her Nose

Cinderella dressed in rose,
Went upstairs to powder her nose.
How many boxes did she use?

Hot Dog

My mother is a butcher;
My father cuts the meat.
I'm a little hot dog
Running down the street.
How many hot dogs did I sell?

Counting-out Rhymes

In a great many children's folk games, one player must be declared *it*—a chaser, a home-base guard, or a scorekeeper. Everybody wants to "be in" first, and nobody wants to be *it*:

> Not I it!
> Not I it!

In order to settle quickly and, more or less, fairly the question of who is to be *it*, children resort to fate. The scapegoat is selected by a counting-out or elimination rhyme. If they are pressed for time, they can be as brief as:

> The lamp is lit
> And you are it!

The chanter-pointer who is a purist will point to a different player for each syllable recited; his paramount concern is fair play. An error in rhythm may provoke cries of "no fair!" or "not fair!" Often however, the chanter manipulates justice a bit either for purposes of suspense or in order to avoid picking a friend or favorite who does not want to serve as *it*. Usually, these feats are managed by skillful alterations in rhythm or by extending the length of the rhyme. The chanter may add a couplet to the existing rhyme:

> My mother told me
> To pick the very best one.

Or several lines:

> Eeny, meeny, miny, mo,
> Catch a rabbit by his toe,
> If he hollers make him pay
> Fifteen dollars every day.
> O-U-T spells out you go
>   (Added lines)
> To Jack's house
> With a dirty dishrag
> In your *mouth.*

The player is eliminated on *mouth* instead of *go,* and the rhyme is repeated until only one player remains.

   Troy State University student collectors discovered that every informant interviewed, including children, their teachers, and other
adult guardians, knew several counting-out rhymes but preferred to
use one or two; and that considerable transmission occurs from one
generation to the next, primarily from older children to younger, and
from teachers to students, as well as wide distribution and exchange of
common rhymes over a large geographical area. The most popular
counting-out rhyme in central and southeastern Alabama is "Eeny,
Meeny, Miny, Mo." Contemporary usage of the rhyme excludes the
formerly common, ethnic name-calling *nigger*, with *tiger* and *rabbit*
dominating the acceptable substitutes. The thirty-odd counting-out
rhymes presented here are, in general, those most frequently reported
by student collectors. Some rhymes are included because of their
significance as variants.
   Many of the jump-rope rhymes, game songs and rhymes, taunts,
riddles, and counting-out rhymes in *Zickary Zan* derive, as does much
of American folk poetry and song, from English nursery-rhyme tradition. The American folk games of children and adolescents, folk
dances, and the play party, evolving out of our English heritage, are all
replete with borrowings, adaptations, and variants from Mother
Goose, who is herself a symbol of the great stream of the Anglo-
American folklore that is primarily verbal in expression. In her songs
may be found all manner of folk phenomena—weather lore, proph-
ecies, superstitions, proverbs, calendars, games, rites, customs, celebrations, and festivals, as well as folk and social history.
   Where, when, and how did all these songs come into existence and
how were they perpetuated? Like all folk traditions, from the four
corners of the earth, from somewhere to everywhere, floating hither
and thither from somebody to somebody, from one day and year and
century to the next.
   While a study of specific survivals, variants, and influences from
Mother Goose in Alabama folklore lies beyond the intent and scope of
this collection, a few examples from these Alabama counting-out
rhymes will demonstrate clearly the relationship of our folk traditions
to that of the English nursery rhyme. "Hickory, Dickory, Dock,"
"Buckle My Shoe," "The Cuckoo's Nest," "Jack," "William
Trembletoe," and "Wire, briar, limber, lock" all derive from Mother
Goose, but what strikes us is the way the folk have varied these traditional rhymes either out of whim or for some definite purpose. These
variations, which include accumulation, substitution, alteration, and
combination, must be understood in terms of the character and practical purpose of the counting-out rhyme in which language and subject
exist fundamentally as rhythmical accompaniment of the counting-
out process, not as rational or poetic meaning. Unlike the riddle, where
verbal distortion and ambiguity constitute the very substance of play,

or nonsense verse, in which language serves to amuse, the counting-out rhyme is a kind of incantation—a ritual overture invested with magical significance—to the game itself. Although the subject matter of counting-out rhymes, both contemporary and traditional, is always related to numbers and counting, the rhythm has the more important role of aiding in the definition of the physical act. Hence, we may account for the presence of so many nonsense syllables and the meaningless aggregate and combination of diverse and unrelated images, diction, figures, and themes within a single rhyme.

As a case in point, the four Alabama variants of "Wire, briar, limber, lock" derive ultimately, according to the Baring-Goulds in *The Annotated Mother Goose* from an American rhyme by Jesse Cochran printed in 1814, which, in turn, is a version of a counting-out rhyme printed in Joseph Ritson's English collection *Gammer Gurton's Garland* of 1784. Astonishingly, Ritson's rhyme has a very near equivalent in one of the Alabama jump-rope rhymes reported to us in the 1960s:

One-ray, two-ray, Zick-ray, a a
One-ray, two-ray, Zick-ray Zan
Halibow, crackabow,
Winbird, swag tail,
Ten bow tan.

Three of the Alabama "Wire, briar, limber, lock" rhymes are built around the Mother Goose rhyme "One Flew Over the Cuckoo's Nest." One contains an allusion to "Hickory, Dickory, Dock," three refer to the Mother Goose "Jack" figure and one to his counterpart, modernized to "Don," and three boast a "dirty dishrag" motif, which may be taken as an emblem of scorn and punishment. Similarly, the six "William Trembletoe" versions combine various motifs and images—the geese and the cuckoo's nest, the fisherman, the hens, the dirty dishrag, old Jack and his house. One of them contains all of these motifs plus "Wire, briar, limber, lock," and still another has been altered to include one of our folk heroes, the railroad man. "Arlie, Barley, Buck, and Doe" does not mention William Trembletoe by name but certainly belongs to his kingdom.

Of the remaining counting-out rhymes—"Eeny, Meeny, Miny, Mo" is the best known in all Anglo-American folk tradition, though it is quite recent; "My Mother and Your Mother" was once a nose game played with young children; "Amen" is widely known as a Southern folk parody sung to the tune of "There'll Be a Hot Time in the Old Town Tonight"; and the nonsense syllables of "Itsy-bitsy soda cracker" obviously reflect Mother Goose influences. Why Jack, the cuckoo's nest, William Trembletoe, soda crackers, the quarreling mothers, "wire, briar, limber, lock," the dirty dishrag, and the mouse of "Hickory, Dickory, Dock" are so prominent in Alabama counting-out rhymes is a bit of a mystery. But here they are:

All in together,
Boys!
One, two, three!

Hickory, Dickory, Dock

Hickory, Dickory, Dock
The mouse ran up the clock.
The clock struck one,
And down he ran,
Hickory, Dickory, Dock.

O-U-T

Hickory, Dickory, Dock
The mouse ran up the clock,
O-U-T spells out goes he to
Old Jack's house with a dirty
dishrag in his mouth, the first
one who shows his teeth is *it*.

Chicago Line

Engine, engine, number nine
Running on the Chicago line,
If the train runs off the track,
Would you want your money back?
Y-E-S spells you are *it*.

One Flew Over

Wire, brier, limber, lock
Three geese in a flock.
One flew east, one flew west,
One flew over the old cuckoo's nest.
O-U-T out goes you, you old dirty
dishrag, you, out goes you.

Dirty Dishrag

Wild briar, limbralock,
Three geese in a flock.
One flew east, one flew west,
And one flew over the old cuckoo's nest.
O-U-T spells out goes he to old Jack's house
With a dirty dishrag in his mouth.

The Old Cuckoo's Nest

Wild briar, limbralock,
Three geese in a flock.
One flew east, one flew west,
One flew over the old
Cuckoo's nest.
O-U-T spells out goes he
to old dirty Don's house.

Wire Briar

Wire, briar, limber, lock
Sat and sang till ten o'clock
The clock fell down,
The mouse ran around.
O-U-T spells out to Uncle
Jack's house,
With a dishrag in his mouth.

Let Him Go Again

One, two, three, four, five
I caught a hare alive;
Six, seven, eight, nine, ten;
I let him go again.

Monkey, Monkey

Monkey, monkey, bottle of beer,
How many monkeys are there here?
One two three, out goes he (she).

Ink Stink

Ink, Stink, bottle stopper,
All out but popper.
O-U-T spell *out* he goes.

I Struck a Match

Everyone puts out both fists. Someone repeats "I struck a match and it
went out," using one word for each fist. The person whose fist receives
a tap on the word *out* puts that fist behind his back. This continues
until all but one person has both fists behind his back. This last person
is *it*.

This process is also used for the two versions of "One Potato" given
below.

Taters

One tater, two tater,
Three tater, four,
Five tater, six tater,
Seven tater, more.

Amen!

One, two, three, the devil's after me.
Four, five, six, he's always throwing sticks.
Seven, eight, nine, he misses every time.
Hallelujah, hallelujah. Amen!

[*Note:* Also in wide circulation as a folk song among children, sung
to "There'll be a Hot Time in the Old Town Tonight."]

Arlie, Barley, Buck, and Doe

Arlie, barley, buck, and doe
Which a way do the fishermen go?
Some go east, some go west
Some go over the old crow's nest.
There's a little tiger boy

What does he do?
Catches his hens, puts them in pens
Some lay eggs, some don't
Go on to ole Jack's house.

Ene, Mene, Miny, Mo

Ene, mene, miny, mo,
Catch a rabbit by his toe,
If he hollers, make him pay
Fifteen dollars every day.

Switten

Mitten, Smitten, Pitten, Switten
Out goes Smitten, in goes Pitten
Out goes Switten and Mitten is it.

My Mother and Your Mother

My mother and your mother were hanging out clothes.
My mother hit your mother in the nose.
What color of blood do you think came out?
B-L-U-E means you are out.

One Potato

One potato, two potato,
Three potato, four,
Five potato, six potato,
Seven potato, *more.*

Mollie Hair

Mollie, Mollie Hair
What cha doin dar?
Settin in de winder
Picking out 'air
Picked out one
Picked out two
Picked out one
Just like you.

Sky Is Blue

One, two, sky is blue
Out goes you!

Dibble-Dabble

Keep the pot a-boilin'
Just for Margie,
One, two, and dibble-dabble
Three.

Itsy Bitsy Boo

Itsy bitsy soda cracker
Itsy bitsy boo
Itsy bitsy soda cracker
Out goes you.

Out Goes You

O-U-T spells out goes you
To the old dirty dishrag's
house.

William Tremble Toe

He's a good fisherman,
Catches hens, puts 'em in the pen
Some lay eggs and some none.

Icky Bicky Soda Cracker

My mother and your mother
Live across the street;
Every night they have a fight.
This is what they say:

Icky Bicky soda cracker,
Icky Bicky boo,
Icky Bicky soda cracker,
Out goes you.

Hanging Out Clothes

My Mama and your Mama was hanging out clothes
My Mama hit your Mama on the nose
Did it hurt?
Y-E-S—out you go.

1918 East Broadway

The people who live across the way,
At nineteen-eighteen East Broadway,
Every night they have a fight and
this is what they say:

Icky-bicky-soda cracker,
Icky-bicky boo,
Icky-bicky-soda cracker,
Out goes you.

A Good Man

William, William tremble toe,
He is a good man, he has hens
that lays eggs for railroad men.
Sometimes one, sometimes two
Sometimes enough for the whole D——crew.
O-U-T out goes you.

Boys a-Plenty

One, two Buckle my shoe
Three, four Shut the door
Five, six Pick up sticks
Seven, eight Shut the gate
Nine, ten A good fat hen
Eleven, twelve A good hoe helve
Thirteen, fourteen Girls a-courtin'
Fifteen, sixteen Girls a-fixin'
Seventeen, eighteen Boys a-waitin'
Nineteen, twenty Boys a-plenty
Twenty-one, twenty-two One for me and one for you.

Some Lays Eggs

William Tremble Toe
He's a good fisherman,
Catches hens, puts 'em in the pen,
Some lays eggs and some none.

Jack's House

William Trimbletoe
Was a good fisherman,
A good fisherman was he.
He catches hens, puts them in a pen.
Some lay eggs and some don't.
O-U-T spells out goes you
To Jack's house with a dirty
dishrag in your mouth.

Some Go East, Some Go West

William, William Tremble toe,
Which way did the fishermen go?
Some go east, some go west,
Some go by the old crow's nest.
There's a little tiger boy.
What does he do?
Catches his hens; puts them in pens.
Some lay eggs, some do not.
Wire, briar, limber lock, settings single
'Til ten o'clock.
O-U-T spells out.
Go on to old Jack's house.

Taunts

One reliable dictionary defines a taunt as a reproach and describes it in terms of the sarcasm and the insult. More specifically, a taunt can be a verbal insult, a tease, accompanied by suitable gestures and facial expressions. Children tend to use it as a substitute for physical violence; insult calls forth reply:

> Sticks and stones
> May break my bones
> But words will never harm me.

And it is not confined to individual use. As a group weapon it is evident at high school football games, where cheerleaders lead the fans in:

> Rickety, Rackety, Rust.
> We're not allowed to cuss;
> But, nevertheless,
> We must confess
> There's nothing the matter with us!

The opposing side may counter with:

> Two bits, four bits, six bits, a dollar,
> All for (team)
> Stand up and holler!
> Yea!

Or, on the playground a group of children may shout together

> Goody-goody gouch!
> Your shirt-tail's out!

A more debasing taunt is the tormentor, generally used by older children, or even by adults, to tease, torture, or otherwise cause a younger child to feel uncomfortable. In this case, the child is tormented because he draws an incorrect conclusion from the use of an unfamiliar word in a familiar context. For example, a child is told that he has ancestors. The child assumes this strange word means a disease, and a disgraceful one, from the tone of voice with which *ancestors* is pronounced, because he knows one "has" chicken pox or the itch. Or when told he slumbered in his bed, the child assumes this verb to be an

adult word for "wet" and is thus tormented by the image of an act he
had thought he had outgrown—or maybe feared he had not outgrown.
This kind of taunt derives its peculiar horror, of course, from the
superior knowledge of the tormentor.

The taunt is not an altogether pleasant aspect of folklore collecting.
The need to inflict pain and insult—the psychology of cruelty—is
subject to much speculation. Nevertheless, the taunt is widely present
in world folklore and is well attested in literature; for example, the
Anglo-Saxon and Homeric boasts are proud statements of ancestry
and past victories in battle. When Unferth taunts Beowulf with a
youthful failure in a swimming match, the hero replies with his own
boastful account. In the *Iliad,* single combat is initiated by an exchange of taunts, and each warrior is distinguished by his own personal war cry, a phenomenon that survives today in American college
battle cries—War Eagle! Roll Tide! The war cry of Achilles is so terrible that it devastates his enemies even before he appears on the field.
Similarly, War Eagle! and Roll Tide! are intended to strike terror in
the hearts of the opponents, but the exchange of these taunts occurs
between the spectators, not the players on the teams.

The taunts presented here exemplify the seductive invitation ("Here
I stand all ragged and dirty / If you don't come and kiss me / I'll run
like a turkey!"), the ethnic jibe, name-calling, the traditional boast of
power with its concomitant challenge, the obscenity, the vulgarism,
and one ridiculous ballad of poor Lulabelle. Even the briefest exami-
nation of this selection reveals affinities with riddles, puns, and the
Yiddish curse. One kind of taunt deserves special attention: the
"What's your name?" exchange. The frequency of its occurrence and
its several variations suggest a deeply rooted aspect of the human
personality—the imperative of self-identity expressed through the literal utterance of a name that, once bestowed, accumulates near magical significance; only, in this case, the real name is not pronounced, but
rather an absurd substitute, Puddentane, Santa Claus, Buster Brown,
John Brown, Hickory Ben Double. Anticipating the questioner's re-
fusal to accept the substitute, the taunter smugly threatens to repeat
the mockery, thereby doubling the humiliation, or to assault the un-
wary victim—slap his jaws, slap or knock him down. So, the assertion
of identity is coupled with insult and challenge. Yet, it ought to be
observed that the enactment of this exchange in children involves little
more than the stylized, playful tease. One child coaches another in the
rhyme, and together they may recite it several times, obviously
pleased with their game. Perhaps it is best to view the taunt in the
kindlier light of children at play, a social amenity refined out of
cruelty, usually a rhythmic and/or rhymed dialogue or statement
intended mostly for fun.

Chants and rhymes are difficult to classify because the folk use them in whatever circumstances or situations they choose. Of the following chants and rhymes, some are more properly considered nonsense verse; yet they often appear in the context of a taunt: "Amen," "Amos and Andy," "All Good Children," "Sally Rand," "Miss Molly," "Sons of Moses," "Miss Sally and Big John," "Across a Steeple," "What Time Is It?" "Johnny's Mad," "Fudge, Fudge," and "Red-headed Peckerwood."

Amen

Amen,
Brother Ben,
Shot a rooster,
Killed a hen.
Hen died;
Rooster cried,
Then committed suicide.

Tattle-Tail

Tattle-tail,
Tattle-tail,
Catch a rat   or   Hang your breeches
and   On a nail!
Grow his tail.

Amos and Andy

Amos and Andy and all stock candy;
When you lick it, you are dandy.

All Good Children

1,2,3,4,5,6,7
All good children
Go to heaven.

1,2,3,4,5,6,7,8
All bad children
Have to wait.

Caught a Fit

____'s it.
And caught (got) a fit,
And don't know how
to get out of (over) it.

Go Away Now

Go away now, don't come nigh me!
Like a kite you have to fly me.
Like a colt you have to tie me.
Happy, frisky Jim!

Sally Rand

Sally Rand,
Lost her fan.
Run, run, run
As fast as you can!

Froggie in the Millpond

Froggie in the millpond,
Can't get out.
Take a stick and
Stir him out.

A Fool's Name

A fool's name
A monkey's face
Always seen in public places.

Order in the Court

Order in the court,
The judge is gotta spit,
If you can't swim,
You shore better git.

Miss Molly

Took Miss Molly out to tea
And on the way back
She tried to squeeze it out
of me.

Ha Ha Hee

Ha ha hee,
Can't catch me,
Can't catch a flea on
a Christmas tree.

Chicken Snot

Chicken snot,
Pick it up and trot,
Go put it in a washpot.

John Brown

What's your name?
John Brown.
Ask me again and I'll
slap you down.

Rather Be Dead

I'd rather be dead
Than red on the head.

Rag Mop

Your hair looks like a mop, a rag mop.

Cross My Heart

Cross my heart and hope to die,
Stick a needle in my eye.

Buger, Buger Bear

Buger, buger bear,
Catch me if you dare.

Here I Stand

Here I stand all ragged and dirty,
Kiss me quick and I'll run like a turkey.

Black and Dirty

Here I stand black and dirty,
If you don't come and kiss me,
I'll run like a turkey.

When I Get Big

When I get big and you get little,
I'm going to beat the fire
out of you.

Jelly

Do you like jelly?
I'll punch you in the belly.

Liar, Liar

Liar, Liar,
Your pants are on fire;
Your nose is as long
As a telephone wire.

Teacher, Teacher

Teacher, Teacher,
I declare
I see Johnnie's underwear.
(or I think I see *your* underwear.)

Double Darn

Darn, darn, double darn,
Triple darn, bang!
Gee whiz, golly, gosh
Gol darn, dang.

Pity the Robbers

I pity the robbers
I pity the crooks
I pity the person who studies
this book.

I See London

I see London, I see France
I see ——'s underpants

Lulabelle

Lulabelle, where are you going?
Upstairs to take a bath.
Lulabelle, with legs like toothpicks
And a neck like a giraffe.

Lulabelle stepped in the bathtub,
Lulabelle pulled out the plug.
Oh my goodness! Oh my soul!
There goes Lulabella down the hole . . .

Glub, glub, glub.

Miss Sally and Big John

Old Miss Sally tell me do,
Is Big John true to you?
If he ain't I'd take his hide,
And take you now for a sorrow ride.

Bushel and a Peck

Caught a fellow in my corn patch.
He had a bushel;
His wife had a peck.
The baby had a roasting ear
Tied around his neck.

Across a Steeple

As I went across a steeple
I met a heep of people.
Some was black, some was blacker,
Some was the color of an ole chew of tobacco.

Buster Brown

What's your name?
Buster Brown.
Ask me again and I'll knock you down.

Puddin-n-tane

What's your name?
Puddin-n-tane.
Ask me again and I'll tell you the same.

Santa Claus

What's your name?
Santa Claus.
Ask me again and I'll slap your jaws.

What Time Is It?

What time is it?
The same time that it was
yesterday at this time.

Hickory Ben Double

What's your name?
Hickory Ben Double,
Ask me again,
And I'll give you trouble.

Up a Hickory

Up a hickory, down a pine,
Split my bretches right behind.

Johnny's Mad

Johnny's mad and I'm glad,
And I know what to please him.
A bottle of wine to make him shine,
And some little girl to kiss him.

Chorus: Johnny is a ninny. (Sing in a singsong fashion and
repeat over and over.)

Fudge, Fudge

Fudge, Fudge, call the judge.
Mammy had a newborn baby.
It is not a girl,
It is not a boy,
It is just a newborn baby.

Cry, Baby, Cry

Cry, baby, cry.
Stick your finger in your eye
And tell your mother
It was I.
Cry, baby, cry.

Fatty, Fatty

Fatty, fatty,
Two by four,
Swinging on the kitchen door.
When the door began to shake
Fatty had a tummy ache.

Red-headed Peckerwood

Red-headed peckerwood,
Pecking on a pine.
Want a chew tobacco,
But you can't chew mine.

Rickety, Rackety Russ

Rickety, rackety, russ
We're not allowed to cuss.
But nevertheless we must confess
There's no one better than us!

Coward, Coward

Coward, Coward,
Buttermilk soured.
Ain't been churned in twenty-four hours.

Ebo, Eyebow

Mabel, Able, inkstink stable,
Ebo, eyebow, bowlegged Mable.

Two by Four

Fatty, fatty.
Two by four,
Can't get through
The bathroom door.
Poor fatty.

Beeswax

In answer to any question:
None of your beeswax, cornbread, and
shoe tacks.

Cheater

Cheater, cheater, red-bug eater!

Go to Grass

Go to grass
and eat pusley!

Icky Backy

Icky backy, soda cracky,
Icky backy boo.
Herman smells, so do you,
And I do too.

★☆☆★☆★☆★☆★☆★☆★☆★☆★☆★☆★☆★☆

Riddles

The riddle exists in Western European folk tradition both as a distinct genre, that is, riddling or the social act of verbal and intellectual play, and as poetic symbol and structuring element in myth, folk tales, ballads, and songs. Many of our oldest Anglo-American folk songs are riddle songs: "Can you make me a cambric shirt," better known as "Parsley, Sage, Rosemary, and Thyme," very widely circulated long before its first appearance in print in the late seventeenth century, presents a series of riddles that symbolize the complexities of love and courtship. To claim the sweetheart, the lover must perform impossible tasks: fashion a cambric shirt without seam or stitches and wash it in a well without water, find an acre of land between the sand and the sea, plow the land with a ram's horn and one peppercorn, reap it with a sickle of leather, and bind up the sheaves with a peacock's feather. The European folk tale of Rumplestiltskin is built on two riddles; the miller's daughter must spin straw into gold (the impossible task riddle), a vicious little old man accomplishes the feat after she has promised him her firstborn, the day of reckoning comes and the miller's daughter, now the queen, bargains for her child and wins by guessing the odd name of the little man (the name riddle or the puzzler) who promptly disintegrates. "Rumplestiltskin" suggests clearly that we pay a harsh forfeit for not solving our own riddles.

Once the riddle lay at the heart of religion and myth; once it was the sign and embodiment of intellectual, mystical, and heroic powers. The priestess at Delphi and the Roman sibyl cast their auguries in the enigmatic language of riddles, ancient Egyptian priests enveloped religious concepts in obscure riddles, and two of our mythic heroes, Samson and Oedipus, are archetypal riddlers. Both the Hebrew and the Greek myths clearly demonstrate the functions of the riddle within the larger forms of the narrative and the drama; moreover, in both stories a riddle initiates and links all the tragic action and is invested with the complex, poetic symbolism of its counterpart, the greater riddle of the tragedy itself.

The mighty Samson slays a young lion with his bare hands, chooses a bride from the Philistines, and on the return to his father's house, finds in the lion carcass a honeycomb, which he eats. At his wedding feast he poses a riddle to thirty companions: "Out of the eater came forth meat, And out of the strong came forth sweetness" (Judges 14:14). The Philistines threaten Samson's wife with death if she fails to find the answer to the riddle. Moved by her weeping plea—if you love me, you will tell me—Samson yields, and on the appointed day the companions cleverly enclose the solution in a counter-riddle: "What is sweeter than honey? And what is stronger than a lion?" (Judges 14:18).

Samson slays thirty Philistines and presents their garments as forfeit to the expounders of the riddle. The Philistines give his wife to one of the companions; thereafter Samson wars against his enemies, eluding every attempt at capture until once again he is betrayed by a daughter of the Philistines, Delilah, who finds out the answer to the greater riddle, the secret source of his strength. Three times she questions him and sets up an ambush, but each time he answers falsely in the manner of a riddle. On the fourth occasion Delilah says "How canst thou say, I love thee, when thine heart is not with me?" (Judges 16:15), and Samson succumbs. The lion riddle now takes on new meaning: Samson is stronger than a lion and his spiritual purity, represented by the uncut hair of the Nazarite, is like the sweetness of honey. His tragic vulnerability to the deceits of love violates that purity and leads resistlessly to his doom at Gaza.

Like Samson, Oedipus is a revered national hero and possessor of acute intellectual powers. He becomes the saviour and king of Thebes by solving the riddle of the Sphinx which afflicts the city with disease and death: What animal crawls on all-fours in the morning, walks upright at noon, and goes on three legs at night? The well-known answer is, of course, man, and it is the greater riddle of man which the Oedipus myth celebrates. Here, although Fate plays a larger role than in the story of Samson, the tragic fall of the hero is a direct result of his overweening desire to sound out all the secrets of his mysterious birth and incestuous marriage, his proud determination to solve the riddle of his own identity. At the last, Samson and Oedipus experience tragic awareness. Samson redeems his people through self-sacrifice, and Oedipus becomes a figure of beneficence and prophecy. He who answers a riddle must "see" the point—as part of their tragic punishment, both heroes are blinded, Oedipus by his own hand, even as Samson dies by his own hand. The lesser riddles they solve, the greater one confounds them. Samson knows the answer but in a moment of weakness surrenders his sacred gift to the enemies of God and thus forfeits his claim to strength; the quest of Oedipus is so passionate that when the overwhelming answer comes, he cannot bear it. We are left with the profound truth which the riddle symbolizes—all of us, like Samson and Oedipus, see and do not see.

The original functions of the riddle within larger narrative and dramatic forms have almost disappeared in written literature. Since the birth of the novel and the modern theater, the riddle of existence has been expounded in a thousand new ways, and it is noteworthy, in this connection, that one of the most popular forms of contemporary fiction, the detective story or mystery, is, essentially, one long, extended riddle. In contemporary folklore, riddles have evolved primarily as entertainment. Riddling as a social act is universal and of great antiquity. Scholars and folklore collectors have gathered riddles from oral tradition and printed sources throughout the world, and for any given riddle there are analogues from many varying cultures. In England folk riddles quickly found their way into print, particularly in nursery-rhyme publications and thereby were perpetuated by generations of children. Oral transmission of riddles, however, remains strong to this day. Riddle warfare between children and adults, among families and friends, was, like charades and acrostics, a popular game at the hearthside and on the front porch in nineteenth-century America. With all sorts of mechanical and electronic amusements so instantly available, it is a bit of a wonder that riddles not only persist but are enormously popular among children and young people who swap them gleefully on the playground, schoolbus, and in the classroom. By now, there is a great body of American riddle lore, and although the true riddle has declined in popularity, the genre has been expanded to include a wide variety of species—puns, wit teasers, jokes, nonsense, trick questions, conundrums, and puzzlers in mathematics and logic. Two major cycles of current adolescent folk humor—the elephant and knock-knock jokes—are comic *who* and *why* riddles; nonsense and shaggy-dog riddles and puzzles flourish everywhere; and parody and satire are widely evident in all the various forms of the riddle.

The reasons for this perpetuation and popularity are not hard to find: riddling is a game of intellectual hide-and-seek, fanciful and playful, which reflects our fascination with secrets and mysteries, our determination to seek out the answer. The folk instinct to riddle is based on the pleasure we take in the manipulation of language and logic, in pulling the wool and the leg, in catching our fellows out, and showing off our own wit. In a very real sense, riddling as a social act is rooted in our fundamental need to know—it is a charming parallel to those tedious and not very well defined intellectual processes by which we come to understand ourselves, to define the physical nature of the universe, and to deal with the vast moral and philosophical complexities of our world. To greater or lesser degree, we all ponder the ultimate riddle of man himself: need we wonder at the existence of millions of small riddles which mirror that single, overwhelming enigma?

The persistence of riddles and riddling leads us to an exploration of their nature. The basis of a true riddle is always comparison of one object to another. Riddles are characterized by deliberate ambiguity, paradox, contradiction, misleading analogy, false deduction, and partially accurate description or induction. The forms of logic are manipulated cleverly to conceal an obvious answer; the witty deception is practiced within a social context in which the listener expects and accepts the skillful trick. Riddles enploy images, concrete details, metaphor, paradox, and contradiction, all of which serve as clues to the answer. These devices, along with rhyme, meter, onomatopoeia, and alliteration, point to the riddle as being one of the oldest forms of poetry as well as entertainment. There are all sorts and kinds of riddles: chain or cumulative riddles; color, size, shape, and form riddles; family relationship riddles; time of year and season riddles; story or narrative riddles; and the "false riddles," enigmas, puzzlers (in mathematics and logic), wit teasers, nonsense riddles, and puns. In all riddles, though, both question and answer are always those common objects and experience with which we are all familiar: the human body (eyes, tongue, nose, hair, feet, mouth, ears, legs), ordinary household items and the affairs of daily living (chairs, shoes, buckets, thimbles, cars, wagons, clocks), plants and animals, (eggs, cows, pumpkins, watermelons, chickens), and the landscape, natural phenomena, and the environment (fire, water, air, churches, houses, graves, roads, hills, mountains, thunder, the sea). Every day the stuff of riddles changes, collections of contemporary American riddles evidence of loss of many experiences and objects of our rural past, wagon tongues, woodstoves, milk buckets, plowing, spinning, drawing, well water, and a gain of new items from our industrial century. Like all folk items, riddles change as the folk change, what is lost by one hand is replaced in the other, and the transformations go on and on in folklore and folk life.

This collection of riddles from Alabama includes true riddles, conundrums, wit teasers, puzzlers, trick questions, jokes, and nonsense. Nearly all of them are in the mainstream of traditional Anglo-American verbal folklore, transmitted and perpetuated orally by one generation to the next. We have printed the answer with the riddle: it is not the element of puzzlement that delights and amuses us. If children are confronted with a new riddle, immediately they answer "I don't know, What?" Not a minute is wasted on mulling; it is the riddle itself they love, or rather its complementary nature, the question and answer delivered almost simultaneously. For children, bless them, there can *be* no riddle without an answer.

Each of these riddles is a treasure handed down lovingly year after year. Around every one thousands of children, teachers, parents, and grandparents are gathered together. Riddles, like all folklore, re-unite us. Their language and logic transform something quite ordinary into a marvel. And, as in all magic, we willingly suspend judgment for a moment, only to cry out "Ah! I should have known!" But we shouldn't have, for therein lies the pleasantry. As Mother Goose says:

> Come riddle me, riddle me, riddle me, ree;
> None are so blind as they who won't see.

As I was going across the field, I met Bill Forgen turning up a lump-a-lump of Thang Bang Borgen. Called Peter Woodskin to bite Bill Forgen for turning up a lump-a-lump of Thang Bang Borgen.

(Bill Forgen was a hog. Thang Bang Borgen was a potato. Peter Woodskin was a dog.)

As I was walking through a field of wheat
I saw something good to eat.
It was neither skin nor bone
And it had none.
(??)

Two brothers we are;
Great burdens we bear.
All day we are bitterly pressed.
Yet this I must say,
We are full all day
And empty when we go to rest.
(Shoes)

Deep as a house, round as a cup
All king's horses can't draw it up.
(A well)

What can go up hill, and go straight and curve?
(A road)

[*Student Collector's Note:* Six legs and two hands down, four legs and three hands up? This riddle is by a lady who wouldn't tell the answer. She made it up herself many years ago, and said that it has to do with the living, the dead, and time.]

What fruit do you find on a dime?
(A date)

What has eyes but cannot see?
(A potato)

What gets wetter the more it dries?
(A dishtowel)

How can you divide 10 potatoes equally between 3 people?
 (Mash them)

What has 18 legs and catches flies?
 (A baseball team)

What is no larger when it weighs 20 pounds than when it weighs 1 pound?
 (Scales)

If you plant a puppy what will come up?
 (Dog wood)

There was an old log, under this old log was an old man, he had three horses, their names was Dapple Gray. Now I've said his name three times and yet you don't know it.
 (Was)

Constantinople is a hard word, can you spell it?
 (I-T)

Can you spell Mississippi?
 (M, I, crooked letter, crooked letter, I, crooked letter, crooked letter, I, humpback, humpback, I)

Can you spell Tennessee?
 (One I see, two I see, three I see, four I see, five I see, six I see, seven I see, eight I see, nine I see, ten I see, Tennessee)

What keys are too big for your pocket?
 (Turkey, monkey, donkey)

White as milk, but milk it ain't,
Green as grass, but grass it ain't,
Red as blood, but blood it ain't,
Black as ink, but ink it ain't,
What is it?
 (Blackberry)

Why did the chicken cross the road?
 (To get to the other side)

Why did the man wear red suspenders?
 (To hold his pants up)

What has four eyes but can't see?
 (A stove)

What has a foot but no toes?
 (A bed)

What has four legs but can't walk?
  (A chair or table)

What is black when it is clean and white when it is dirty?
  (A black bowl)

Two legs sat up on three legs with one leg on its lap?
  (A man sitting on a three legged stove with a leg of mutton on his lap)

Belly to belly with the sun to their backs
a little piece of meat to fill up the crack?
  (An old sow lying in the sun with pigs sucking)

How many letters in the alphabet? (The answer will usually be 26.)
  (No, the angels said "Noel" [no L] so there are 25.)

He wears his cap upon his neck,
Because he has no head.
And he never takes his cap off
Until you're sick in bed.
What is it?
  (Medicine bottle)

If two is company and three's a crowd, how much is four and five?
  (Nine)

Make a sentence with these words: Deduct, Defence, Defeat, and Dehead.
  (Deduck went over Defence and Defeat went before Dehead.)

Red within, red without,
Four corners round about.
  (A brick)

What has a mouth and can't talk, four down standing and switch
about?
  (A cat)

As I was going across the bridge, I met a man.
He had hammers, he had nails, he had ten cattails.
If I tell his name, I'll be the blame,
For I told his name five different times.
What was his name?
  (His name was I.)

What has a thousand eyes but can't see?
  (A tea strainer)

What has eight eyes and can't see, a tongue and can't talk, and a soul
and can't be saved?
  (A shoe)

Water over water, and water under water. What is it?
(A woman walking across a bridge with a bucket of water on her head)

What's white or brown when it goes up and yellow when it comes down?
(A raw egg)

You're a pilot on a jet bomber. You receive your instructions to go 800 miles west; 1,800 miles south; 200 miles north; and 1,000 miles east. Then go 100 miles up, and come back down again. What's the name of the pilot?
(You)

Why is cooking exciting?
(It has many stirring events.)

How does a witch tell time?
(On her witch watch)

What did one ghost say to the other ghost?
(Do you believe in people?)

What can speak all the languages in the world?
(An echo)

What animal is most likely to eat a relative?
(An anteater)

Two sheep behind a sheep, two sheep in front of a sheep, and a sheep between two sheep. How many sheep are there?
(Three)

Railroad crossing, look out for cars. Can you spell it without any "R's"?
(I-T)

What is black and white and red all over?
(A newspaper or a sun-burned zebra)

Why do ducks fly south in the fall?
(It's too far to walk.)

Which side of a pitcher is the handle on?
(On the outside)

What is the difference in here and there?
(The letter T)

What has 8 legs and sings?
(A quartet)

Long legs and short thighs,
Bald head and no eyes.
    (A pair of tongs)

A riddle, a riddle
I suppose;
A hundred eyes
And never a nose.
    (A sieve)

What goes all day, sits in the corner at night with its tongue hanging
out?
  (A shoe)

What runs all day and never walks,
Often murmurs, never talks;
Has a bed and never sleeps,
Has a mouth and never eats.
    (A river)

Who may marry many a wife and yet be single all his life?
  (A preacher)

Two and one shoe polish
Three and four machine oil
Four and one is what?
  (Five)

Why is it bad to write on an empty stomach?
  (It isn't so bad, but paper is better.)

What is it that grows larger the more you take away from it?
  (A hole)

Sally in the pea patch
picking up peas
Along came a bell cow
Sally's kicking up her heels.
  (Sally is a cow and the bell cow is a rattlesnake.)

What is the surest way to keep fish from smelling?
  (Cut off their noses.)

What did one wall say to the other?
  ("We'll meet at the corner.")

What did the rug say to the floor?
  ("I've got you covered.")

Poke out its eye and it has nothing left but a nose. What is it?
  (Noise)

What is it that nobody wants but wouldn't give up if he has it?
(A bald head)

What is it that goes all over the house in the daytime and stands in the corner at night?
(A broom)

What has ears and can't hear?
(Corn)

What has a body and can't breathe?
What has a body and can't talk?
(A wagon)

If you were in a room with no windows nor doors, what would you do?
(Strike out.)

Why do hens lay eggs?
(If they dropped them they would break.)

What goes up when rain comes down?
(An umbrella)

What is the difference between a train and a teacher?
(A teacher says to throw away your chewing gum, and a train says choo-choo.)

What can a volcano do that a human can also do?
(Blow its top.)

If a boy ate a green apple what would his telephone number be?
(8 – 1 – Green)

What goes up but never comes down?
(Your age)

If you were walking down the street, and your toe got smashed, what would you do?
(Call a tow truck.)

Why do humming birds hum?
(Because they don't know the words.)

What's live on each end and dead in the middle?
(A man plowing with a mule)

What's white with a red nose, the longer it stands the lower it grows?
(A white candle)

What walks all day and talks all day, lies down at night but never sleeps?
(A cowbell)

What bites and never swallows?
(A frost)

What walks all day, sits in a corner at night, but never sleeps?
(A pair of shoes)

What does a chicken do when it stands on one foot?
(Holds up the other one)

What creature eats less than any other?
(The moth, it eats holes.)

What kind of bird has wings, but can't fly?
(A dead bird)

A man was put in jail, and another man came to see him. But he wasn't allowed to visit the prisoner, and when the prisoner insisted, they asked if the visitor was kin to him. He replied, "Brothers and sisters I have none, but this man's father is my father's son." Who was the visitor?
(He was the prisoner's father.)

What has more lives than a cat?
(A frog, it croaks every night!)

Why do they name hurricanes after girls?
(Well—you never have heard of a he-a-cane, have you?)

When is a boy like an angry duck?
(When he stands on his head—[his down is up].)

What is big at the bottom, little at the top, something in the middle goes flippity-flop?
(A churn)

Nebuchadnezzar, King of the Jews, spell it with two letters and I'll give you a pair of shoes.
(I-T)

What's black when it's clean and white when it is dirty?
(Blackboard)

What is white and thin and red within, with a nail at the end?
(Finger)

What is a bottomless vessel to put flesh and blood in?
(Ring)

What has neither flesh nor bone but has four fingers and a thumb?
(Glove)

What does a diamond become when it is placed in water?
  (Wet)

What did the big rose say to the little rose?
  (Hiya Bud.)

What did the sock say to the shirt in the washtub?
  (Meet me at the clothesline, that's where I hang out.)

First white,
Then red,
Two days old,
Then dead.
  (A cotton bloom)

What will run down a hill but not up?
  (Water)

What goes through a pane of glass without breaking it.
  (Sunlight)

What walks with its head down?
  (A nail in a shoe)

What is the difference between a jeweler and a jailer?
  (One sells watches and the other watches cells.)

What is the difference between a pretty girl and a mouse?
  (One charms the he's and the other harms the cheese.)

What is the difference between an old dime and a new penny?
  (Nine cents)

What is the difference between a man and a hen?
  (A man can lay an egg on a red hot stove without burning himself and a hen can't.)

What did the dresser say to the table?
  (I see your legs. So what: I see your drawers.)

What is it that doesn't ask questions, but must be answered?
  (A telephone)

There were three flies in the kitchen, which one was a cowboy?
  (The one on the range)

What are the kindest vegetables?
  (Cabbage and lettuce—they have big hearts.)

Why are clouds like coachmen?
  (They hold the rains.)

Why are cowardly soldiers like candles?
  (When exposed to fire, they run.)

How is a tree like a dog?
  (It has bark.)

What animals do you always take to bed?
  (Your calves)

Riddles Collected by Ruby Pickens Tartt

Ruby Pickens Tartt of Livingston, Alabama, was the most extensive
collector of that Alabama folklore gathered by the National Writers'
Project of the WPA during the 1930s. These riddles are filed with the
Alabama WPA folklore collection on deposit at the Library of Congress.

  (A man was to be hanged. He was told that if he could ask them a
riddle which no one could answer he would be set free.)
    A horn eat a horn
    Up a high oak tree.
    If you unriddle this
    You can hang me up.
The answer: A man named Horn up a tree eating a horn.

    As I was goin' over London Bridge
      I met a man
      Had ribbon
      Had rings
    Had er heap uv pretty things:
    Had a hammer nine ten
    Had a hammer ten ten
    Tripple Jack blow the bellows
    Through the old sheep shank
    Through the Molly full of peppers
    Such a riddle never known.
The answer: Box of matches.

    It opens like a barn door,
    Has ears like a cat.
    Guess all your life time
    You can't guess that!
The answer: A man's vest.

Four fingers and a thumb
Neither flesh nor bone.
Answer: a glove.

Hitty Titty, upstairs
Hitty Titty, downstairs
Don't mind, Hitty Titty
Will bite you.
Answer: a wasp.

Go in stiff and bricky
And come out limbee drippy.
Answer: greens.

White drove White out of White.
Answer: A white man drove a white cow out of a white cotton patch!

Nonsense Verse and Parodies

In its highest literary form, parody is a device of satire. Whatever the level—vulgar, adolescent, or sophisticated—it is dependent upon imitation: one must know the original before the parody can be successful. In fact, it is the juxtaposition of the original and the parody that elicits laughter. Long ago Aristotle correctly observed that children learn primarily through imitation. They are instinctive mimics yet, in their earliest years, not conscious of their own mimicry. Somewhere, somehow, at least by the end of the first grade, they discover imitation as amusement; they mock the mannerisms, facial expressions, and speech of their teachers, classmates, and parents, knowing full well that they put their little backsides in peril. The parodies we collected, both from elementary and high school students, are humorous take-offs on familiar songs, "Battle Hymn of the Republic," "On Top of Old Smokey," "The Star-Spangled Banner," "Yankee Doodle," and "America." The most popular of these satirize the teacher, the principal, and school:

> Mine eyes have seen the glory of the coming of (teacher)
> She was coming around the corner in a souped-up Model A
> One hand was on the throttle
> And the other on a bottle
> Of Pabst Blue Ribbon Beer.
> Glory, Glory Hallelujah
> Teacher hit me with a ruler.
> I knocked her over the beam
> With a rotten tangerine
> And her teeth came marching out.
> Hup 2, 3, 4, 5, . . .

> My eyes have seen the glory of the burning of the school,
> We have trampled all the teachers,
> And we've broke the Golden Rule,
> We marched into the office and we scattered everything,
> And the Rats go marching on.

Parodies of Mother Goose rhymes are common:

> Mary had a little lamb
> She lived in Alabama
> It followed her to school one day
> And I hit it with a hamma.

A good many reflect recent history: the Model A, the Ford Psalm, World War II (going to see the king of Germany whose name is Mickey Mouse), and the cartoon figure Popeye, not nearly so popular now as in the 1940s and 1950s. Strictly speaking, these parodies are not survivals of a traditional folk culture, but they are transmitted orally, and their instinct and flavor are truly folk.

Nonsense is a prominent characteristic of American folk humor. Our comic songs and ballads, tall tales, pranks, and jokes are replete with the merriment of exaggeration, distortion, absurdity, and outright lies. Man's instinctive need for play is clearly evident in these nonsense verses that circulate widely among children and adolescents. The nonsense oration was popular on up until the 1950s, and even now at family gatherings somebody may rise to the occasion and recite one. Knock-knock, elephant jokes, and shaggy-dog stories are contemporary folk expressions of nonsense, and there doesn't seem to be any end to the ridiculous twists and turns young people keep inventing.

Nonsense is a delight. We derive pleasure from it precisely because it is nonsense, and yet often there is much sense in nonsense. It does much more than entertain us; it tells the truth upside down, hind part before, wrong side out. The inexplicable is not always fearsome, and exorcism of demons need not always be a darkly serious rite; charms may be amusing as well as solemn. Nonsense is such a charm, the outermost reaches of the comic spirit, man abandoned to play, and—as Lewis Carroll, Edward Lear, and Mother Goose plainly teach us—man willfully restructuring his world into a topsy-turvy creation. Illogicality, absurdity, wild extravagances, impossibilities, reverses, incredulities, irony, and flat contradictions of fact are hallmarks of nonsense:

> One bright day in the middle of the night
> Two dead men stood up to fight:
> Three blind men to see fair play,
> Forty mutes to yell hooray.
> Back to back they faced each other,
> Drew their swords and shot each other.

These Alabama nonsense rhymes are distinguished by their sharp visual images, pungent folk speech and nomenclature, verbal ambiguity, and ridiculous situations. Notable too is the evocation of a strong sense of our rural past—chinches and bedbugs, a mule named Jenny, chickens and bread trays, a fiddling sow and her dancing pigs, Granny's "teakittle," and jaybirds dying with the whooping cough. Like the other verbal folklore items in *Zickary Zan*, these nonsense rhymes and parodies bring us back home.

NONSENSE VERSE

Bobby

Bobby went down to the ocean
Bobby went down to the sea,
Bobby broke a milk bottle,
And blamed it on me,
I told Ma,
Ma told Pa,
Bobby got a licking,
Ha, Ha, Ha!

Marco Polo

Marco Polo went to France
To teach the ladies how to dance;
First a kick, then a bow,
Marco Polo showed them how.

Marco Polo went to France
To teach the ladies the hootchy-kootchy dance;
Heel, toe, around we go,
Turn your back to the old potato sack!

One Bright Day

Ladies and gentlemen; dogs and cats; bowlegged mosquitoes and cross-eyed bats: I stand before you because I can't stand behind you, to tell you a story I know nothing about.

One bright day, in the middle of the night, two dead boys got up to fight. Back to back they faced each other, drew their swords and shot each other. The deaf policeman heard this noise and came and shot the two dead boys. If you don't believe this lie is true, ask the blind man, he saw it too.

Teakittle

The thunder roared and the lightning flashed,
Broke old granny's teakittle all to smash.

Chicago

Chicken in the car and the car won't go,
That's the way to spell Chicago.

Jenny

I had a little mule, her name was Jenny;
When I bought that mule she cost me plenty;
But I sold that mule for one little penny;
And now I have neither the penny nor Jenny.

Bullfrog

The funniest sight I've ever seen,
Was a bullfrog sewing on a sewing machine,
He sewed so fast, and fine, and wide,
He sewed a polecat's tail to a tomcat's hide.

New York

Knife and a fork and a bottle and a cork,
That's the way to spell New York.

Tim

I had a little dog, his name was Tim;
I put him in a bathtub to see could he swim;
He drank all the water and ate all the soap
And almost died with a bubble in his throat.

Bedbugs

Ashes to ashes, dust to dust,
If the chinches don't get you
The bedbugs must.

I Love Me So

I love myself, I love me so,
I took myself to the picture show,
I put my arms around myself,
And hugged myself to death, by heck.

When I Was a Little Boy

When I was a little boy about so high,
Ma would take a little stick and make me cry,
Now I'm a big boy and Ma can't do it,
Pa takes a big stick and goes right to it.

Did You Ever?

Did you ever go a-fishing on a hot summer day
Sitting on a log—the log rolled away?
Put your hands in your pockets,
Your pockets in your pants,
Did you ever see a fish do the hootchy-kootchy dance?

Chewing Gum

I stood in a corner chewing gum,
Along came a tramp and said he wanted some,
No, you dirty idler,
No, you dirty bum,
You ought to have a lickin'.

Death of the Old Cat

Roses are red, violets are pink,
The old cat died in the kitchen sink.

Shot a Rooster

Amen, Brother Ben
Shot a rooster and
Killed a hen.
The hen died and
The rooster cried
Ben committed suicide.

Jaybird

Way down yonder not so very far off
A jaybird died with the whooping cough.
He whooped so hard with the whooping cough
That he whooped his head and tail right off.

Away Down Yonder

Away down yonder in the forks of the branch
The jaybirds whistled while the buzzards danced.

Away down yonder in the forks of the branch
The old sow fiddled while the pigs all danced.

Laugh

Laugh, I thought I'd die.
Die a funeral;
Funeral, flowers;
Flowers, money;
Money, work;
Work, me work!
Laugh, I thought I'd die!

Fight and Scratch and Tarry

I'm on my way and I ain't got long to tarry,
Old folks love to fight and scratch,
Young folks love to tarry.

Possum up the Persimmon Tree

Possum up the persimmon tree
Rabbit's on the ground
Rabbit says "You trifling scoundrel,
Shake them simmons down."

The raccoon's tail has rings all around;
The possum's tail is bare.
The rabbit has no tail at all,
Just a little bunch of hair.

[*Note:* Stanzas are widely current in various American folk song and dance cycles.]

Rover

I had a dog,
His name was Rover;
When he died,
He died all over;
All but his tail,
And it turned over.

Pete and Repeat

Pete and Repeat sitting on the fence,
Pete fell off and who was left?
Repeat.

Pete and Repeat sitting on the fence,
Pete fell off and who was left?
Repeat.

Etc.

Pretty Little Boy

Mary's mad.
And I am glad,
And I know what will please her:
A jug of wine
To make her shine
And a pretty little boy to squeeze her.

Billy Booster

Billy, Billy Booster
Had a little rooster;
The rooster died and Billy cried,
Poor little Billy, Billy Booster!

Last night and the night before,
Twenty-four robbers came to my door.
When I went down to let them in,
They knocked me down with a rolling pin.
Ten ran east, and ten ran west,
And four jumped over the cuckoo's nest.

Ballad of Elbert County Jail

I was standing on the corner,
Doing no one harm.
Along came a policeman,
And took me by the arm.
He took me to a little box,
And rang a little bell.
Along came a little car,
And took me to my cell.
At six o'clock in the morning
I looked upon the wall,
The bedbugs and the cooties
were having a game of ball.
The score was 6–0.
The bedbugs were ahead.
The cooties knocked a home run
And knocked me off my bed.
At seven o'clock in the morning
The jailman came around.
He brought me bread and coffee
That weighed about a pound.
The coffee tasted like turpentine.
The bread was very stale,
And that's the way they feed you
At the Elbert County Jail.

Jelly-Cake

As I was walking near the lake,
I met a little rattlesnake;
He ate so much of jelly-cake,
He made his little belly ache.

Wee Wa, Petty Saw

Wee Wa, petty saw
Jack Moore Jenkins
Can you shoe a horse of mine?
Yes Sir, that I can,
Good as any other man;
Bring him in the stall
One nail drives all,
Wee Wa, petty saw
Jack Moore Jenkins.

No, My Child

Mamma, mamma, may I go down to the corner to meet my
beau?
No, my child you may not go down to the corner to meet your
beau.
Daddy, daddy, may I go down to the corner to meet my beau?
No, my child you may not go down to the corner to meet your
beau.
Grand-pa, grand-pa, may I go down to the corner to meet my
beau?
Mamma and daddy said I can't go down to the corner to meet
my beau.
Tell your ma to hold her tongue, she went out when she was
young.
Tell your pa to do the same, he is the one who changed her
name.

Old Aunt Pearly

Old Aunt Pearly likes sugar and tea
And old Aunt Pearly likes candy,
Old Aunt Pearly can dance all around
Swing anyone that comes handy.

Chicken in the Bread Tray

Chicken in the bread tray
Scratching out dough
Mammie, will your dog bite?
No, child, no.

[*Note:* These words often appear in the song "Skip to My Lou."]

Dr. Peck

There was an old doctor whose name was Peck,
He fell in a well and broke his neck.
I will not weep, I will not moan.
He ought to tend the sick and leave the well alone.

An Old Man in Peru

There was an old man in Peru,
Who dreamed he was eating a shoe,
He woke up in fright in the middle of the night.
And found it was perfectly true.

The Hole

I had a nickel,
I walked around the block,
I walked right into a baker's shop,
I took two doughnuts right out of the grease,
And handed the lady my five-cent piece.
She looked at the nickel,
And she looked at me,
And said, "This money ain't no good to me,
There's a hole in the middle and it goes straight through."
Says I, "There's a hole in the doughnut too."

The Old Goose and the Gander

Way down yonder in Grandma's lot,
The old goose laid and the gander sot,
Gosling died,
The old goose laughed.
And the gander cried.

A Little Beau

I have a little finger
I have a little toe;
When I get a little bigger,
I'll have a little beau.

Farmer's Love Letter

My darling sweet (potato)! Do you (carrot) all for me? My heart (beets) for you and my love is soft as a (squash). I am for you strong as an (onion). You are a (peach) with your (radish) hair and (turnip) nose. You are the (apple) of my eye, so if we (cantaloupe) then (lettuce) be married, for I know we will make a happy (pear).

Spiders and Fireflies

I woke up Monday morning,
I gazed upon the wall.
The spiders and the fireflies
Were playing a game of ball;
The score was ten to twelve,
The spiders were ahead,
The fireflies knocked a home run,
And knocked me out of bed!
I went downstairs to breakfast,
The bread was hard and stale,
The coffee tasted like tobacco juice,
Right out of the county jail.

PARODIES

At the Bar
(Tune: "At the Cross")

At the bar,
At the bar,
Where I smoked my first cigar,
And the money from my pockets rolled away.
It was there by chance
That I tore my Sunday pants
And now I have to wear them every day.

My Country's Tired of Me
(Sung to tune: "My Country 'tis of thee")

My country's tired of me,
I'm going to Germany
To see the king.
His name is Mickey Mouse
He runs a boarding house
On every mountain side
You can see his rule abide.

Oh, Say Can You See?
(Tune: "Star-Spangled Banner")

> Oh, say can you see
> Any redbugs on me?
> If you can, pick a few,
> And you will have red bugs, too.

Sugar Bowl
(Tune: "Jesus, Lover of My Soul")

> Jesus, lover of my soul,
> Lead me to the sugar bowl,
> If the sugar bowl is empty,
> Lead me to my mother's pantry.

Over Hill, Over Dale
(Tune: "The Caissons Marching Song")

> Over hill, over dale
> We have hit the dusty trail . . .
> (Cough, Cough)

Glug, Glug, Glug
(Tune: Navy theme song)

> Anchors away, my boys,
> Anchors away . . .
> (Glug, glug, glug)

Crash!
(Tune: Air Force song)

> Off we go, into the wild blue yonder . . .
> Crash!

Mockin' Bird
(*Cf.* folksong "Hush Little Baby")

Mama, mama, have you heard—
Daddy's gonna buy me a mockin' bird.
If that mockin' bird don't sing,
Daddy's gonna buy me a diamond ring.
If that diamond ring gets broke,
Daddy's gonna buy me a billy goat.
If that billy goat don't bray,
Daddy's gonna buy me a bundle of hay.
If that bundle of hay gets wet,
Daddy's gonna give me a spanking I bet.

Yankee Doodle

Yankee Doodle went to town
Riding on a scooter.
Hit a bump,
Skint his rump,
Landed in the city dump.

Lohengrin

Here comes the bride
Big, fat, and wide,
See how she wobbles
From side to side.

Shotgun Shells

Jingle bells, shotgun shells
Rabbits on the run.
Oh, what fun it is to ride
In a one-horse Model A.

The Ford Psalm

The Ford is my master; I shall not live in peace.

It maketh me to be down in both mud and dust; it leadeth me in the path of grease.

It restoreth my license dues; it leadeth me in the paths of shame and disgrace for its name's sake.

Yea, though I go through the dark shadows of the night, Thou art with me; the jolting of thy springs maketh me to ache.

Thou preparest a string of bills in the presence of mine creditors; thou anointest my head with oil; my wrath runneth over ever.

Surely if this thing follow me all the days of my life I will dwell in the house of the insane forever.

From the Halls Of Montezuma

From the halls of Highland View
To the shores of St. Joe Bay,
We will fight our teacher's paddle
With spitballs and bubble gum.
If they send us to the principal
We will whip and throw him out.
Then we'll call everybody
And let all the children out.

My Country 'Tis of Thee

My country's tired of me
I'm going to Germany
To see the king.
He drives a whiskey truck
And he lives in the dump,
And he is very drunk,
Yes, very drunk.

John Brown's Ford

John Brown's Ford had a puncture in its tire
John Brown's Ford had a puncture in its tire
John Brown's Ford had a puncture in its tire
And he patched it up with chewing gum.

One Dern Eggplant

Mary, Mary quite contrary
How does your garden grow?
With silver bells and cockleshells
And one dern eggplant.

Let Me Call You Sweetheart

Let me call you sweetheart,
I'm in love with your limousine.
Let me hear you whisper
That you'll buy the gasoline.
Keep the headlights glowing
And both hands upon the wheel.
Let me call you sweetheart,
I'm in love with your automobile.

Tor-e-a-dor
(Sung to Toreador's Song from *Carmen*)

Tor-e-a-dor don't spit on the floora
Use the cuspidora that is what it's fora.

Riding on a Turtle

Yankee Doodle went to town
Riding on a turtle.
Turned the corner just in time.
To see a lady's girdle.

Redbug Stew

O say can you see any redbugs on me?
If you can, pick a few
And we'll have redbug stew.

Popeye

I'm Popeye the Jailor Man
I live in a garbage can.
I eat all the lizards
I'm Popeye the Jailor Man.

Davy Crockett

Born on a mountaintop in Tennessee.
The ugliest creature you ever did see.
Killed three nurses and that ain't all
Drowned the doctor in alcohol.
Davy, Davy Crockett
Wanted in New Orleans.

Little Chicken
(Tune: "Turkey in the Straw")

Oh, I had a little chicken in our backyard,
She couldn't lay an egg but she tried awful hard,
So I ran hot water up and down her leg,
Oh, the little chicken cried and the little chicken begged,
And the little chicken laid a hard-boiled egg.

I had another chicken in our backyard,
She couldn't lay an egg but she tried awful hard,
When the preacher came for the folks to see,
That chicken entered the ministry.

New Teacher
(Sung to tune of "Old Smoky")

On top of Old Smoky
All covered with sand
I shot my new teacher
With a green rubber band.

I shot her with pleasure
I shot her with pride
On top of Old Smoky
She tanned my hide.

Bowlegged Women

I'm Popeye the sailor man,
I live in the spinach can,
I eat all the gizzards
And spit out the lizards,
I'm Popeye the sailor man.

I'm Popeye the sailor man,
I live in the garbage can,
I love to go swimming
With bowlegged women,
I'm Popeye the sailor man. Toot! Toot!

I Don't Like Navy Life

Biscuits in the Navy,
They say they're mighty fine,
One rolled off the table
And killed a friend of mine.

Chorus:

Oh, I don't want no more Navy
Gee, but I want to go home.

Chicken in the Navy,
They say it's mighty fine,
Give you fifty dollars
Take back forty-nine.

Coffee in the Navy,
They say it's mighty fine,
Good for cuts and bruises
And tastes like iodine.

Shows in the Navy,
They say they're mighty fine,
Ask for Betty Grable
They give you Frankenstein.

Shoes in the Navy,
They say they're mighty fine,
Ask for number sixes
They give you number nine.

Clothes in the Navy,
They say they're mighty fine,
I need Lana Turner
To fill out part of mine.

[*Note:* A World War II comic protest song which Richard Dorson, who has collected it in *American Folklore*, calls "the most representative folk song of that era." It is performed by Oscar Brand on Vol. 3, LP 1420, Riverside, of *Everybody Sing*. The chorus is especially well known.]

★☆★☆★☆★☆★☆★☆★☆★☆★☆★☆★☆★☆★☆★☆★☆★☆★☆★☆★

Autograph Albums

Nowadays young people inscribe their names, greetings, and compliments on pages of high school annuals, but in the late nineteeth and early twentieth centuries sweethearts and friends wrote verses in autograph albums. We reprint here the contents of two such albums, both from the Burton family of Tallapoosa and Elmore counties, both dating from the 1890s.

The first belonged to Mrs. Ruth Herren's sister, Miss Minnie Burton, its various authors being friends, schoolmates, brothers, sisters, and cousins of the young lady to whom they wrote. The second, now in the possession of Mrs. Jim (Ruth Herren) Hornsby of Tallassee, Alabama, a niece of the Burton family, was apparently shared by all the Burton sisters.

Like nineteenth-century tombstone epitaphs, autograph writings are unashamedly sentimental. In fact, these slim velvet- and leather-bound volumes are collections of sentiments—affectionate tributes, oaths and protestations of friendship, wishes and prescriptions for a happy life—though some of the writings are markedly comic and even satiric. Their burden is Time and Eternity, and their answers to those awesome riddles are Memory and Friendship. The admonition "Remember Me" occurs again and again, more than any other phrase, and the words are written with full, melancholy awareness of forthcoming separation, both temporary and ultimate. Hence, the test of friendship becomes remembrance—we seek a reality in the minds of others, an existence not subject to the laws of time and space. Autograph verse, which resembles that of greeting cards, especially valentines, is not, of course, poetry; admittedly the species is most often trite and mawkish, yet an actual reading from these yellowed pages of faded, exquisite penmanship evokes sincerity. Bright hopes, deep trusts, faithful friendships appear in the very crossings of T's, the florid curves of capital letters; and every once in a while somebody strikes off a really fine phrase: "May a shadow never come before thee."

Many of these verses were popular folk items of the nineteenth century, originating who knows where, circulating in almanacs, newspapers, and magazines, but some of them were original with the Burton clan and their friends. One may still purchase autograph albums, but they have fallen from grace, though in the 1950s and 1960s children were fond of "slam books," school composition books converted to another use: the practice of writing nasty comments about classmates and teachers—more innocent than not, however. The verse itself survives in greeting cards, a billion-dollar business in America, and in the custom of the autograph seeker who wants the celebrity-hero's magical name coupled with his own, a perfunctory "Best Wishes" sometimes thrown in for boot. The human need for memory and friendship is poignantly exemplified in these treasured albums of autograph verses and signatures.

The editors wish to thank the Burton family, Mrs. Herren, and Mrs. Hornsby for permission to reprint these family albums.

From the Autograph Album of Miss M. Burton, Tallapoosa County, Alabama, 1891–1896

This album is now in the possession of Mrs. Ruth Herren, Tallassee, Alabama. We have tried to make a faithful transcription of the originals, though the penmanship and age of the manuscripts presented some obstacles.

> *To Miss Minnie Burton:*
> This book to you is tendered,
> from your sister, sincere and true,
> hoping but to be remembered,
> when I'm far away from you.
> > Your Loving "Sister,"
> > MAGGIE BURTON

> Miss Minnie
> _____

> Accept dear friend
> these lines from me,
> they show that I remember
> thee and hope each line
> some thought retain 'til
> you and I shall meet again.
> > Respectful J. N. BA

> Miss Minnie
> In the days and years
> of the future may you
> contain much happiness
> and when you are departed
> from this world may God
> crown you with a crown of life
> ——best wishes for you
> > ——BURTON

Your friend——
R. H. Culledge
Daviston, Ala.
July 8, 1895.

Lost yesterday somewhere
between sunrise and sunset two
golden hours, each set with sixty
diamond minutes, no reward is offered,
they are lost forever.

Lovingly,
Lula.

Miss Minnie,
Forget me not, forget
me never till yonders
bright sun shall sink
forever.

Your friend,
W. B. W.

Miss Minnie,
Dear friend, remember me
when far away and only
half awake. Remember
me on your wedding day
and send me a piece of
your cake.

Your True Friend
W. E. S.

Miss Minnie please
forgive me for what
I've just done.

R. H. G.

Lavinia Fuller
            is a sweet girl

Miss Minnie
May you live happy each
day of your life get and
make a good wife.

Your friend
J. H. G.

Feb. 26, 1895——

To Miss Minnie
My wishes and my hopes for
you. Find glad expression here.
Although, indeed its very true,
there is no room for all that's due.
                    Your friend
                G. H. Langley

Arise, Ala.
August 14th/23
May a shadow never come before thee

"Sweet little Minnie"
"Remember me"
        ——— —

        ——— —

        ——— —

certainly
May life be to thee
a long summer day.

Miss Minnie
Dr.
I hope that your faith
may be a bed of flowers
and that your life may
be a life of endless pleasure.
                Your true friend
                    ——Harwell

Dear Minnie,
Remember your friend,
        Annie—— [?]
            Daviston, Ala.
Aug. 96

    As sure as comes your
wedding day a broom to you
I will send in sunshine use
the brushy part in storm the
the other end.
                A. E. S.

There is a little flower that
blooms around the cot it whispers
in the sunshine dear Minnie "For-
get-me-not."
>>> Your devoted cousin
>>>>> LAVINIA FULLER

Long may you live
Happy may you be
Sitting on the
woodpile thinking
of me.
>> Your sincere coz
>>>> ANNIE——[?]

Remember me early,
Rember me late,
Remember me as your
own; School-mate.
May 6th, 1892. CLARA B. WOODDY

To Minnie
May life be to thee
one long summer day.
>>> Your true friend
>>>>> A. P. S.
June 29th, 1894

Minnie Burton
My dear sister
Remember your brother
>>>> JAMES
June 2/1895

Dear Cousin
When sailing down the
stream of life in your
little bark canoe may
you have a pleasant trip,
with just room enough for
two (2) Your cousin E. B.

Your friend
> [JAMES?] STILL"
Marcook, Ala.
?/14/95

Dear Cousin
I cannot wish thee greater
divine joys than others here
expressed but I respond with
every power *To wish thee ever*
blessed.
                    EUGENE BURTON
Denver Ala. Feb. 14, 1893

Remember me as one who loves
only you now and forever, but
alas! I know not my fate
ever and ever I shall keep
on relying on your kind heart
to make me happy always.
1-7-95

Dear Minnie
Leaves may wither,
Flowers may die,
Friends may for*sake* thee,
But *never* will *I*.
              Your *sincere* cousin
                    MAMIE FULLER
Dec. 29th, '92

Miss Minnie
May happiness be thy lot,
And peace thy steps attend,
Accept this tribute of respect.
From one who is thy friend.
                        Truly yours
                        G. H. L.

May the flowers of love
Encircle your home
Through this many
A year to come.
Remember me by day,
Remember me I say.
     A. P. McCLANDON

To a friend,
Since then no hour has past
Hast made life more sweet,
And even strangers happy
Whom thou didst kindly greet,
    Your true friend
     LUTIE OLIVER

Dear little friend
In memorys golden chain
Regard me as a link.
    Your friend
     A. D.

Dear Minnie——
Fall from the highest window
Fall from the cliffs above
Fall '' '' highest mountain
But don't you fall in love.
     Your cousin
    ELLA G. BURTON
Princeton [?]

Miss Minnie
May your face, ever shine
as pure and bright as it
does now, and never bear no
trace of trouble, in this life.
Then, at death may shining angels
bear your noble soul to the spirit
land. Is the wish of your friend

To Miss Minnie
Remember well and keep in mind,
that a good true friend is hard to find
and when you find one just and true
change not the old one for the new.
     B. W. BURNETT
Dudleyville Dec. 20, 1891

2+ + (w or u) or xx u b
I see u or xx *for me*
I am.
   MISS CRENSHAW
    JAMES BURTON
  Denver Ala.

Dear cousin
True friends are like
diamonds, precious but rare,
false ones like autumn leaves
found every where.
    In fond rememberance
        YOUR COUSIN

One torn, [indecipherable] page

From the Autograph Album of the Burton Sisters: Kate, Ella, Lucy, Maggie, and Bessie, Tallapoosa County, Alabama, 1895–1905

The album is now in the possession of Mrs. Jim Hornsby, Tallassee,
Alabama.

I looked for my love,
This wide world through,
I looked in my heart
And found there you.

I need not write to tell the tale,
My pen is doubly weak.
Oh! what can idle words prevail,
Unless the heart could speak.
        Yours '10derly
          L. G. BURTON
"And not at homework was I"

When days are dark,
And friends are few
Remember me
And I will you.
      Your friend,
        G. H. S.

Be not the furth [fourth]
Friend to him
Who has three
And lost them.
        A. M. C.

When friends forsake thee,
And loved ones love you not,
Then remember cousin Maggie,
That Mamie is the *truest* coz.
You've got.

May 9th, 1893   EUGENIA
                 Shady Dell

Feb. 19th- 1898
  So long as you live in this world alone,
  Never forget *Mama* and loved ones at *home*.
                       JAMES M. BURTON

  Love me little
  Love me long,
  Is the burden of my song.
May 13, '95   MINNIE LOU

When other lips and other hearts,
Their tales of love shall tell,
In language whose excess imparts
The power they feel so well,
There may perhaps in such a scene,
Some recollections be,
Of days that have as happy been,
Then you'll remember me.

Miss Kate
  The road is wide you
  cannot step it I love you
  and you cannot help it.
                  Your friend
                  G. H. SMITH

May your Days
  be days of peace
  and slide along
  as slick as grease
    This Dec. 27, 1900

You are the
meanest boy
I know.
  LUCEY BURTON

May you be happy each day
of your life get a good
husband, and make a good wife.
          Is the wish of your
          Sister ELLA BURTON
Jan. 28, 1905

    My Maggie
The waters may rise
    and rocks may fall
    but my love for you
    will last through them
    all, your friend
July 29/95   W. B. W.

Miss Lucy Burton
        Dearest Fr
Think of me when
you are happy keep
for me one little
Spot in the depth of
your affection
Plant a sweet for-
get me not
          Your True Fr
          ANNIE MCEACHEN

Dear Lucie —
Tis sweet to be remembered
But sad to be forgot
So let me to you whisper
Dearest one forget me not
                Yours in love
                LIZZIE BUSBEE
Cusseta
Ala

My Dear Lucie
When you get old and can
not see put on
your specks and
write a line to
    me
          Your Sister
          BESSIE

I remain your
[The remaining three lines consist of strange illegible script, perhaps abbreviations or some kind of shorthand, followed by dashes across the page. The entry is unsigned and undated.]

When rocks hills and distance
divide me and you no more I
see Just take your pin and paper
and write a line to me
>> Yours truly
>> G. R. TALBOT

Always remember
> Your truest friend,
>> LULA
La Fayette, Ala.
> June 4, 1(8)95

Dear Kate

When days are dark and friends
are few Remember me and
I will you
>> Your Sis
>> BESSIE B

Miss Lucie Burton is my best girl
If there ever was
a pretty girl, in this
world it is Lucy
Burton for she is
all ways in a whirl
>> Your coz
>> ARCHIE HERREN

Dear Bessie
> Remember when far far off
>> Your sister
>> ELLA B.

Miss Lucy Burton
Remember me when far
far off
Where the woodchucks die
> with the whooping cough.
>> WWS

Sigh poor heart
and do not weep,
'Tis better
to die and
be at rest,
than to sigh
for him a
gain

    M. Annie Burton
        La Fayette
              Ala.
5/8/95
    Is sweet old girl

Within this book
    so fine and white
    let none but friends
    presume to write.

This July 11th, 1900
When this you
see remember
    me

When the march winds blow
And water is low, Remember
me Kate, where ever you go
        JIM BUZBEE

9 chicks & ducks

Remember me
When this you see
And I will remember
you at the sea.

In the golden chain
    of memory
Regard me as a
    link.
        Hard Times
"Exactly so."

Lucie Burtons Darling fellow

Oh, Oh

Miss Lucie,
    Remember me when
I am far a way!
          Your friend
          A. L. SMITH
I certainly do remember you,
and you are *always far away.*

Dear Sister,
    May the wings of your happiness
never lose a feather.
            R. P. BURTON
            La Fayette
               Ala
7–3–95

On the broad highway of
    action
Friends of worth are far and few,
But when one has proved
    her friendship,
Cling to *her* who clings
    to *you.*

Dear Coz-
       In after years when you recall
The days of pleasures past,
And think of joyous hours and all
Have flown away so fast
When some forgotton air you hear
Brings back past scenes to thee
And gently claims your listening ear,
Keep one kind thought of me-
            Your coz-
            T. P. BURTON
April 29th, 1895

Miss Lucie Burton
  May the golden bells
  of memory often
  vibrate the name
  of your friend
                    SANDERS
12/30/97

Dear Cousin-
      May your
future life be as bright and
joyous as mine and Your future
will be haunted with Sunshine.
                    T. P. BURTON

Dear Schoolmate:
      Today is only a
grand time to prepare for the
great, but uncertain *tomorrow.—*
it may be for eternity.
            Sincerely,
                Your friend
                    RHG—

Daviston Ala
July 8, 1895

When on this page you
look think of the one that
wrote his name in this
Book.   JIM
1–9/98

Miss Maggie
      Remember me
Your true friend
      J. A. C.
this the 26th day of Feb 95

Time and tide wait
for no man.

Bessie Burton
My love for you is such
a weight I have
to ship it by
the crate.
"SHO MISS KATIE"

Autograph Rhymes Collected by Students At Troy State University

When this you see, remember me.
Remember the boy who wrote upside down.
Remember the boy from town,
Remember the boy from the country,

When you get married and have twins,
Don't come to me for safety pins.

Remember well and bear in mind,
A jaybird's tail sticks out behind.

Sure as a rat runs along the rafter.
You are the one I am after.

Roses are red and violets are blue.
Sugar is sweet and so are you.

I love coffee
I love tea
I love pretty girls (boys)
And they love me.

I love you naughty, I love you nice,
I love you like a cat loves mice.

I love you little, I love you big,
I love you like a little pig.

As sure as the vine grows round the stump,
You're my darling sugar lump.

When you get married and live on a hill,
Send me a kiss by a whip-poor-will.

The river is wide,
And you can't step it.
I love you,
And you can't help it.

Remember well and bear in mind,
A true friend is hard to find.

If on this page you chance to look
Just think of the writer and close the book.

Cows love cottonseed,
Dogs love meat,
I love you
Because you're sweet.

Way back here out of sight,
I write my name just for spite.

And from a curious little fortune-telling book presented to Mrs. Lucy Solomon in 1921 by her sister "Hennie":

Long may you live,
Long may you tarry,
But, child, whatever you do,
Mind who you marry.
                    Your friend,
                    MCP

★☆★☆★★☆★☆★★☆★

Folk
Say

★☆★☆★★☆★☆★★☆★

Proverbs and Similes

The folk speech we collected in Alabama falls into two broad divisions—proverbs and similes. Like the traditional games of children, folk say actively preserves our past. When we utter a proverb like "First hen to cackle laid the egg," we unconsciously memorialize a way of life that no longer exists except in isolated geographies. The objects and experiences that are the substance of folk speech derive from a rural landscape, and yet they survive in a mechanized century. Why do these old sayings spring effortlessly, without will or thought, to our lips?

What we preserve and what we discard in folklore, and why, are difficult questions but, at least with folk say, some answers can be suggested. First, these Alabama sayings have become idioms, a convenient oral shorthand instantly understood by speaker and listener. Second, their structure, diction, and substance are all mnemonic in nature. Like the superstition (and some of these are statements of superstitions) they may consist of two balanced or contrasted parts:

> A penny saved is a penny earned.
> Go to bed singing, get up a'crying.
> If you want your dinner, don't offend the cook.
> Who has not courage should have legs.

Alliteration and rhyme often make them easy to remember:

> April showers bring May flowers.
> Don't burn your bridges behind you.
> A bit dog always barks.

Finally, these Alabama folk sayings survive because they are invested with all the vibrancy of our folk life. Their images and metaphors derive from the very substance of our history and landscape, the ordinary objects, events, and happenings of our daily lives: mighty oaks and acorns, goose and gander, milk cows and mole hills, brooms and bridges, kettles and frying pans, bats and ticks, fiddles and feathers, mules and haystacks, dippers and baskets. Visually, they are sharp and clear:

Spiders gather in the house of a gossiper.
As nervous as a cat on a hot tin roof.
Gold shines in the mud.

Their language is redolent of ordinary folk conversation—vivacious, direct, immediate:

Every eye shut ain't asleep.
Beauty don't boil the pot.
You can't catch a possum with your dog tied.

Quite often their wisdom and poetry are based on keen, repeated observation of familiar natural phenomena and human behavior:

A burnt child dreads the fire.
A short horse is easy curried.
As full as a tick.
As blind as a bat.
Empty wagons always make the most noise.

Many are wonderfully comic, relying on hyperbole, distortion, nonsense, and ridiculous images:

As fine as frog hair split three ways.
If it don't rain, it'll be a long dry spell.
My shoe soles are so thin, I could step on a dime and tell if it's heads or tails.
He is so cross-eyed, when he cries the tears run down his back.
It rained hard enough to choke a frog.
As hot as a June bride in a feather bed.
She's got freckles on her—but she's pretty.
So bowlegged she can't hem up a hog in a ditch.

Teachers of freshman composition make all-out war on clichés like "sharp as a tack," "quick as lightning," "clear as a bell"; yet a study of these similes reveals that they are absolutely *right*: the essence of any given object is most appropriately, unerringly selected, the abstraction rendered clearly and vividly—the fairness of a lily, the dryness of a bone. Although we must oppose hackneyed thought and trite speech in student writing, perhaps it is not totally absurd to teach the nature of metaphor through the folk similes with which students are already familiar. Curiously enough, such expressions recover some of their original vitality when we really look at them.

The wit, wisdom, and experience of the human race have been compressed into proverbs throughout our history, and there are numerous collections in world literature. Many American proverbs and maxims stem from the Bible, Shakespeare, and Ben Franklin's *Poor Richard's Almanack*. In Carl Sandburg's *The People, Yes*, the short sayings of the American people become their poetry as well as their folk wisdom. Once upon a time and not too long ago, either, proverbs were recited to children in dead moral earnest: "Pride goeth before a fall," "Pretty is as pretty does," "Don't cut off your nose to spite your face." Nowadays, they are offered simply as reflections or comments on human behavior. Proverbs are often based on metaphor, hence their full meaning is readily apparent. They are designed to tell us truth, to offer advice based on previous experience, to guide us in making moral choices, to show us the practical outcome of human situations; they reflect the major concerns of our life: money, sex, love, death, pain, punishment, work. They teach us patience, discipline, forbearance, and humility in plain, common-sense speech, not by abstruse arguments in philosophy and theology. The awful thing is we don't listen, we don't learn, and we keep doing exactly what the proverb warns against. Its meaning never comes home to us until we've finished with the forbidden. Ah well, we're never too old to learn, and tomorrow's another day. And, besides, proverbs confuse us, one contradicts the other. Is it absence makes the heart grow fonder? Or, out of sight, out of mind?

A wise old owl lived in an oak,
  The more he heard the less he spoke.
    The less he spoke the more he heard.
      Why can't we be like that wise old bird?

Two heads are better than one, even if one is a sheep's head.
What's sauce for the goose is sauce for the gander.
Eye for an eye, tooth for a tooth.
Mighty oaks from little acorns grow.
Penny-wise; pound foolish.
You can't make a silk purse out of a sow's ear.
Rob Peter to pay Paul.
Let sleeping dogs lie.
You can get too much of a good thing.
Where there's smoke there's fire.
Clothes don't make the man.
I put my foot in my mouth.
When he says rabbit, she hops.
I swear on a stack of Bibles this high.
There's a chip on your shoulder.
This knife is so dull it wouldn't cut hot butter.
He's too big for his breeches.
Hold your horse.
I've got a bone to pick with you.
If the shoe (or cap) fits, wear it.
It's raining cats and dogs.

She gives me the heebee-jeebees.

I'll knock you so high in the air, you'll starve to death coming down.

He can turn around on a dime.

All I know I keep forgetting.

A still pig drinks the slop.

An ounce of prevention is worth a pound of cure.

A penny saved is a penny earned.

Honey will catch more flies than vinegar.

A penny for your thoughts.

Don't put off till tomorrow what you can do today.

They live from hand to mouth.

Every cloud has a silver lining.

A bit dog always barks (or hollers).

He who lives by the sword, dies by the sword.

Think twice before you speak.

The only way to have a friend is to be one.

The reward of a thing well done is to have done it.

Say what you think, but think before you say it.

Empty wagons always make the most noise.

Better to laugh at nothing than never to laugh at all.

A girl threads a needle by putting the thread through the needle's eye; a boy
    does the same by putting the needle eye over the thread.

Two can live as cheap as one, but only for half as long.

A bird in the hand is better than two in the bush.

If wishes were horses, beggars would ride.

People who live in glass houses shouldn't throw bricks.

A lie stands on one leg, truth on two.

To err is human, to repent divine, to persist devilish.

Glass, china, and reputation are easily cracked and never well mended.

A watched pot never boils.

Curiosity killed the cat—but satisfaction brought him back.

What goes over the devil's back will come back under his belly.

Didn't know them from Adam's house cat.

I'd stretch a mile if I didn't have to walk back.

Well—that's a deep subject for such a shallow mind.

Well—is in the ground.

Don't cut off your nose to spite your face.

You can't sell the cow and have the milk.

Don't bite off more than you can chew.

Let every man skin his own skunk.

Barking dogs never bite.

You can't have your cake and eat it too.

Give him an inch and he'll take a mile.

Out of the frying pan and into the fire.

Put the big pot in the little, and boil the legs off the dumplings.

The higher you climb, the greater will be your fall.
Every eye shut ain't asleep.
Don't make a mountain out of a mole hill.
Every dog has his day.
Too many cooks spoil the broth.
His bark is worse than his bite.
If you go to bed with dogs, you'll wake up with fleas.
Ask me no questions and I'll tell you no lies.
One rotten apple spoils the whole barrel.
You can't teach an old dog new tricks.
Haste makes waste.
As luck would have it.
Pretty is as pretty does.
Better late than never.
Poor but honest.
Give a man an inch and he thinks he is a ruler.
Worry is like a rocking chair. It will give you something to do, but it won't get you anywhere.
In the summertime, a morning rain is like an old lady's dance, it is soon over with.
Don't stick anything in your ear any smaller than your elbow.
The bigger they are the harder they fall.
An idle mind is the devil's workshop.
The ornament of a house is the friend who frequents it.
The clock struck 12:00 and kept striking. The old lady said, "Old man, get up—it's the latest it's ever been."
It rained hard enough to choke a frog.
When it rained it was a young Noah.
It's a long road that never turns.
Money doesn't grow on trees.
Come hell or high water.
Age before beauty.
Practice makes perfect.
Everything that shines isn't gold.
A new broom sweeps clean.
April showers bring May flowers.
Beauty is only skin deep.
A chip off the old block.
Never too old to learn.
Tomorrow's another day.
It's better to be safe than sorry.
Don't burn your bridges behind you.
Don't cross your bridges before you get to them.
Praise the bridge that carries you across.
Don't take any wooden nickels.

Two spoons in the kettle spoil the soup.
Step on a crack and break your mother's back.
Love unwisely given, brings sorrow to the giver.
Found money don't ever bring pleasure.
Spiders gather in the house of a gossiper.
Out of the mouths of babes . . .
Six of one, half dozen of another.
Great day in the morning.
Leaping lizards.
By George . . .
Devil take the hindmost.
By the skin of my teeth.
In the twinkling of an eye.
Little did I think . . .
Method in my madness.
As poor as a church mouse.
As thin as a rail.
As fat as a pig.
As brave as a lion.
As spry as a cat.
As bright as a dollar.
As weak as a rat.
As proud as a peacock.
As sly as a fox.
As fair as a lily.
As cross as a bear.
As neat as a pin.
As quick as (greased) lightning (or a whip).
As ugly as sin (or homemade sin).
As dead as a doornail.
As white as a sheet.
As flat as a pancake (or flounder, or flitter).
As red as a beet.
As crazy as a loon.
As brown as a nut.
As blind as a bat.
As mean as a miser.
As full as a tick.
As sharp as a needle (or a tack).
As clean as a whistle.
As hard as flint (or nails).
As bitter as gall.
As fine (or fit) as a fiddle.
As clear as a bell.
As dry as a bone.

As light as a feather.
As hard as a rock.
As stiff as a poker.
As calm as a cucumber.
As green as grass (or a gourd).
As busy as a bee.
As good as gold.
As round as a butterball.
As hungry as a bear (or wolf).
As slick as glass.
As black as smut (or the ace of spades, or a pot).
As old as Methuselah.
As meek as a lamb.
As stubborn as an ox (or mule).
As straight as a board (or an arrow).
As tall as a pine.
As yellow as gold.
As slow as syrup on a cold morning.
As tough as whitleather.
As big as a bear (or elephant).
As hard to find as a needle in a haystack.
As fine as frog hair split three ways.
So hot it burned the hair off my tongue.
As tight as Dick's hatband.
As drunk as Cooter Brown.
As thick as thieves.
As thick as hairs on a dog's back.
As hot as a depot stove (or firecracker, or fox).
As nervous as a cat on a hot tin roof.
As hot as a June bride in a feather bed.
As pretty as a picture.
As mad as an old wet (or setting) hen.
As happy as a lark (or a pig in a turnip patch, or a dead pig in the sunshine).
So hungry I could eat a dog.
So bowlegged she can't hem up a hog in a ditch.
So bowlegged he can't stop a cow from running between his legs.
Sour enough to make a pig squeal.
Swell up like a bull.
Panting like a lizard setting on a hot rock.
Caused as much excitement as a new rooster in the henhouse.
Like a long-tailed cat in a room full of rocking chairs.
Like a blind dog in a meat house.
Like a bull in a china shop.
Straight as a martin to his gourd.
Barefoot as a haint (or hound dog).

Sorry as gully dirt.
Not worth a tinker's dam.
Too wet to plow.
Too much sugar for a dime.
There is more than one way to skin a cat.
Whatever happens twice, happens three times.
Stitch in time saves nine.
Make hay while the sun shines.
She's the salt of the earth.
Whistling girl and a crowing hen never came out to no good end.
Whistling woman and a crowing hen is enough to run the devil out of his den.
All work and no play makes a very dull day (or Jack a dull boy).
How's your better half?
If the ox gets in the ditch on Sunday, get him out.
Sweep around your own back door before you sweep around someone else's.
Go to bed singing, get up a-crying.
An apple a day will keep the doctor away.
Feed a cold, starve a fever.
Rub it on blue, it will come true.
A man is known by the company he keeps.
I can't never did.
Can't squeeze blood out of a turnip.
Wait broke the wagon down.
Beauty don't boil the pot.
A rolling stone gathers no moss.
If you want something done, do it yourself.
Don't let your right hand know what your left is doing.
What your mind don't know, your heart don't grieve after.
Shut the door. Were you raised in a barn?
Use your head for something besides a hatrack!
The customer is always right!
There is more truth than poetry in that.
Life is what you make it.
I found it last place I looked.
The luck of a lousy calf.
Don't you wish you had been born rich instead of so good-looking?
Let me put a bug in your ear.
What wind brought you here?
It won't be long now.
The worst is yet to come.
Got bus left?
Oh, I got my news by the grapevine.
What you don't know won't hurt you.
The grass is always greener on the other side of the fence.
Practice what you preach.

Figures don't lie, but liars can figure.
A bad penny always comes back.
You can't tell a book by its cover.
Better be dead than out of fashion.
No matter how thin the cake batter, there is always two sides.
Happy is the bride the sun shines on.
A man of words and not of deeds is like a garden full of weeds.
She's got freckles on her—but she's pretty.
If it don't rain, it'll be a long dry spell.
Sit the milk bucket under the bull.
Musta went around by Gabe's (or Price's).
You all come when you feel like it.
Are you coming to the shindig?
Come and fetch knitting.
Bill and Sally jumped the broom yesterday.
They got hitched a while back.
Darkest hour is just before day.
When want comes in the door, love flies out the window.
Some folks don't know how well off they are, until they try to do better.
Easy street is hard to find.
To get nowhere, follow the crowd.
None is so blind as he who won't see.
Patience is an old maid waiting to be married.
Don't count your chicks until the eggs hatch.
Like father, like son.
Enough is sometimes too much.
It's better to be silent and be thought dumb than to speak and remove all
    doubt.
Don't judge others with your own yardstick.
Time and tide wait for no one.
Honesty is the best policy.
When it rains, it pours.
The way to a man's heart is through his stomach.
A son is a son until he takes a wife; a daughter is a daughter all the days of her
    life.
There is no fool like an old fool.
Never look a gift horse in the mouth.
Take care of the pennies and the dollars will take care of themselves.
Who steals my purse steals trash.
Birds of a feather flock together.
There's many a slip twixt the cup and the lip.
The love of money is the root of all evil.
Where your treasure is, there will your heart be also.
If you want your dinner, don't offend the cook.
He who has seen little, marvels much.

You can lead a mule to water, but you can't make him drink; and you can force a man to shut his eyes, but you can't make him sleep.

As a twig is bent, the tree grows.

Beggars must not be choosers.

Everybody's business is nobody's business.

Keep your mouth shut and people may think you are a fool; open it and they will know it.

Gold shines in the mud.

Who has not courage should have legs.

Six feet of earth makes all men equal.

Poverty makes thieves, love makes poets.

A burnt child dreads the fire.

I'd rather be a live coward than a dead hero.

Do not put all your eggs in one basket.

He is so ugly, he has to slip up on the dipper to get a drink of water.

He is so cross-eyed, when he cries the tears run down his back.

My shoe soles are so thin, I could step on a dime and tell if it's heads or tails.

He is so tight, he squeezes the nickel so hard he makes the Indian ride the buffalo half the time.

Let the buyer beware.

You can't catch a possum with your dog tied.

Absence makes the heart grow fonder.

Out of sight, out of mind.

Two wrongs do not make a right.

Willful waste makes a woeful heart.

Between the devil and the deep blue sea.

Between a rock and a hard place.

A haughty spirit goeth before a fall.

A fool and his money are soon parted.

Where there is a will there is a way.

First hen to cackle laid the egg.

Love is like the moon, when it doesn't increase, it decreases.

A short horse is easy curried.

The ground flew up and hit him in the face.

There is always a nut in every family tree.

The sky is the limit.

★☆★☆★☆★☆★☆★☆★☆★☆★☆★☆★☆★

Appendixes

★☆★☆★☆★☆★☆★☆★☆★☆★☆★☆★☆★

Schoolteachers' Diary

While we were editing these volumes, we came upon an unusual document, a journal kept by the principal and teachers of a school in Tallapoosa County during the fall term of 1893. The first page announces that it is the "Diary of Alex City Graded High School." The manuscript, which occupies two ledgers, has deteriorated, but the entries are remarkably legible. Once the property of Miss Mattie May Pearson, Alexander City, Alabama, whose father, J. M. Pearson, served as principal of the school, it is now in the possession of her nephew, Jacob Walker, an attorney in Opelika, Alabama. We are grateful to the Pearson family and to Mr. Walker for allowing us to print several excerpts from this journal.

The country school is no more. Whatever the legal, political, and social aspects of a transformed rural America, the folklorist cannot but be a bit saddened by those changes, for the school, the store, and the church functioned as social centers for the rural folk. Children exchanged taunts and riddles, learned ancient games, songs, chants, and rhymes in the schoolyard and classroom; grown folks told tales and swapped yarns in front of the store, and in the church cemetery lay carved stones that yielded the sum of their lives.

This is not to argue against urban contemporary folklore—much has been and more is forthcoming in the study of, for example, subway and sidewalk graffiti, the folkways of prison and the university campus, the language and lore of C.B. radio. A folk will forever have changing lore and ways, but the difficulties in demonstrating the relationships between the lore of 1893 and 1976, in charting the adaptations and changes that occur in transmission or in explaining the obscurity or even loss of certain folk elements, are enormous. Where and why does a particular folk song survive, relatively intact, over two centuries? Why is it so difficult to teach the old English circling dance "Go In and Out Your Windows" to thirty-one children of a second grade class in 1980?

These selections from the Schoolteachers' Diary will, perhaps, help us answer those questions, and they will be of interest to teachers, administrators, historians, and older readers who can remember what it was like to recite Cicero around a potbellied stove on a cold, dreary November day. While there is little evidence of folklore genres in these

entries, they provide amusing and informative glimpses of a turn-of-
the-century Alabama school, of a milieu in which most certainly the
charts, riddles, rhymes, tales, and games of our grandparents
flourished. It is precisely this kind of supportive evidence the folklorist
ought to examine in order to make sense of what he finds, to understand the culture that produced a game such as "Crazy Liza," though,
as yet, we've found nobody who played it or knows anything about it.

The entries are remarkably frank, considering the fact that all
teachers wrote in the same ledger and that the entries were read aloud
to pupils, other teachers, and, on one occasion, to the city council. They
run from September 11, 1893, the day school opened, to September 14,
1894, when they break off, with no explanation. The entries from
December 11–14 are dated 1894, but apparently the year given is in
error, since the narrative flow is uninterrupted. Some time during the
day, all the teachers wrote in the journal. (The second ledger is an
account book with sums of money listed opposite pupils' names.) That
is, they all wrote, except Miss Susie Sutton, the piano and music
teacher, who seems to have forgotten and, twice, turned in her entries
weeks later. The teachers include: J. M. Pearson, the principal, who
taught the higher forms, and whose observations are nearly always
characterized by a high moral sense and an ardent belief in the neces-
sity and values of schooling; S. T. Pearson, who often notes his own
transgressions as well as those of his students, and who, in spite of
some gloomy thoughts on man's innate, stubborn evil, appears to be
sincerely committed to the doctrine of educability; Miss Susie Sutton,
always pleased with her students and their gifts to her, good-natured,
and jolly; Miss Fannie Hebr, teacher of Latin, English, and grammar,
wry, sharp witted, stern and kindly, who always writes her entries in
verse, sometimes moral or sentimental, but generally satiric and en-
tertaining; Miss Hattie Perryman, a storybook teacher of the younger
children, genuinely delighting in her charges, her love for teaching
aglow in every entry. Subjects mentioned in the journal include:
Geometry, Latin, English, Practical Grammar, Spelling, Geography,
Physiology, Civics, History, and Mental Arithmetic. The school day
began with assembly or "exercises," moral instruction, announce-
ments, religious observances (prayers, Scripture reading, and short
sermons, often by a local minister), and songs. Pupils went home for
"dinner," and often many were tardy for afternoon sessions. That the
school was "progressive" is indicated by at least two subjects—
physiology and civics. That it reached back to mid and early
nineteenth-century educational philosophy is also clear from the
prominence of Latin.

Girls clamor for spelling matches, and debates are a weekly affair.
Altogether, the temper of the school is one of warmth and good will on

the part of both teachers and students. The teachers do despair now and then, but not of behavior, rather of their pupils' failure to learn. Generally they are amused and charmed by minor infractions of discipline codes, and they never fail to rejoice when students do good work.

We wonder what sort of schoolteachers' diary might be kept today.

Diary of Alex-City Graded High School
(Fall Semester, 1893)

Monday, Sept. 11—1893.

The good little boys thus honored me,
To show their love, each took his place,
Where nearest he could view his teacher's face.
To me it seemed, that each one thought
His love last year I had truly bought,
For with looks so radiant, frank and sweet,
I knew no call need I repeat.

Miss Fannie Hebr

School opened with 94 children in attendance. The teachers are ready for work, and the bright, cheerful children are also ready to do their duty. Capt. A. G. Grant, Artist for the Central R.R. System, came over and introduced himself as Mr. Grant. He took a picture of the school in the afternoon. We spent the day in organizing.

S. G. Pearson
Tuesday, Sept. 12—1893

The boys were good, but laws have we,
They have forgotten so much since June in '93.
Not only in books—; I will not complain,
But briefly explain,
It is not that the boys do not care;
They only forgot that I was there.

Miss Fannie Hebr

All classes were heard, the children worked beautifully all day, but made considerable noise by dropping slates and working with their desks.

Miss Hattie Perryman

Wednesday, Sept. 13, 1893

One new pupil   Eunice Walker failed on a problem in Algebra and cried about it. Belle Branch spent the evening with us. Ada Street missed everything in History.

J. M. Pearson

Alas for me! As sure as three times three are nine,
   The boys do not think that they are mine,
Although I roar and stomp and scream;
   Whatever I say, they think I do not mean.
                                       Miss Fannie Hebr

All seemed to be more settled and were very peaceable and quiet.—
the lessons were very good. The little drill exercising in counting
money, writing and map making were much enjoyed, and I received
such quantities of flowers from the little ones.—both morning and
noon.
                                       Miss Hattie Perryman

Thursday, Sept. 14—1893.
One new pupil. Brag Algebra Class failed, History class had good
lesson.
Stephen Pearson tried to eat goobers on the sly during study hours.
Annie Horn is absent on account of being sick.
                                       J. M. Pearson

Friday Sept. 15,—1893
Ella Polk missed all of her History lesson. W. J. Harlan spent the
evening with us. One girl gave me a saucer of ice cream to excuse her
for being tardy, and the pupils allowed me to eat it in the room. Marvin
McLendon only objected.
                                       J. M. Pearson

Have had better order and some improvement in lessons today. My
last Arith. class did well this after-noon. One of the girls said I was
"likered up" so to-day they came near not knowing me. But the trouble
is, my face is so bare. For a moment this Aft.noon, Willie Pearson
looked as if he could eat a stalk of millet.   S.G.P.

Monday, Sept. 18—93.
We have nine new pupils present, making the roll 111. Marvin
McClendon fell asleep at his desk. Lizzie Wilder, Annie Christian, Lake
Parker, Chas. Brewer & Hez. Street were appointed teachers for the
Brag Algebra Class, and were given two pupils each.
These five teachers were the only members of the class who had
solved all the problems. Earnest Walker is absent.
                                       J. M. Pearson

Wednesday, Sept. 20.
Bro. Brewer conducted the religious exercises. Miss Hebr's Caesar
class knew absolutely nothing about their lesson. History class had
good lesson.
Lessons better than yesterday. Nina Little absent afternoon on account of sickness.
                                       J. M. Pearson

History class nearly all failed,—about four exceptions. Three failures in Ment. Arith. Lesson in Pract. Grammar both interesting & instructive.

Emmett Ogletree looked in his book "on the sly" in Pri. Grammar class. Clara & Donee Pearson couldn't define a simple number in Ment. Arith. Class.

S. G. PEARSON

Thursday Sept. 21.
Nina Little & Eunice Walker absent. Willie Coley wanted to know the difference between Mother-in-law & Stepmother. Lessons very good. Oliver Bachelor failed to spell sugar. He said shu. No water in well.

J. M. PEARSON

Several members of class in Pract. Arith failed on examples. Chas. Brewer talked in Gr. Class. In Elocution Class Buford Dean, Emmett Ogletree, Otho Calvin, Bennie Estes, Albert Polk, & Chas. Adams tried to talk "on the sly". Chas. Pearson failed in Arith.

S. G. PEARSON

Nothing unusual to-day. Lessons very good. Extracted one tooth for Sydney Herzfeld—believe I'm getting to be quite a dentist.

MISS HATTIE PERRYMAN

Friday, September 22, 1893
The children have been good today, and have thought I have been *very sour*. An effort on my part to keep better order has impressed them with the idea that I "got up wrong" this morning. We have had good order and fair recitations to-day.

S. G. PEARSON

Robbie B. thought with his lesson to grapple.
Was quite out of the question, he's eat a crabapple.
This as he found, was love's labor lost.
But at very small cost.
With the apple in his mouth and the book in his lap.
His teacher presented him with a neat facial slap.

MISS FANNIE HEBR

Monday, Sept. 26.
Bro. McCoy conducted the Religious exercises. Six new pupils, making roll 117. Some of the pupils had "Sunday-fever," but I had no trouble in getting them to shake it off. Eunice Walker tardy after dinner. Lessons average. Tom Floyd absent.

J. M. PEARSON

After opening exercises I called for news. P. Y. Willis gave an account of the opening of the Cherokee strip of land between Kansas & Oklahoma, and the great rush of the people to secure homes. Several members of Pract. Grammer class failed in parsing. Some of the large girls & boys have never learned *how* to sit down. Chas. Adams, Albert Polk, Willie Morre, Emmett Ogletree, Jno. Grimsley, Lola Motley, & Otho Calvin failed to have their compositions in grammar class.

S. G. PEARSON

After recess, Willie Stearns ran away home to hunt the cow,
that thought it fine sport to roam.
But he, trembling, came back slowly, but soon;
May be he saw the cow jump over the moon.

MISS FANNIE HEBR

Sept.   [The late entry of Miss Susie Sutton, Music teacher]
The piano came to-day. It created quite a sensation among the children. They came flocking in at recess to see it. It is a pretty upright, Fischer piano, with an ebony case, and has a sweet tone. The first to take lessons on it seemed to enjoy the honor very much.

Monday, Oct. 2—1893.
Had eight new pupils to-day, making roll 125. The threat of last Friday has been executed, and new schedule has been arranged. New pupils, new books & new work have filled us with new life, & this morning we take fresh courage & resolve to do our best. Prof. W. B. Neighbors made us a short visit & conducted one recitation for me. Pupils have done well today.

J. M. PEARSON

Tuesday, Oct. 3

Although from our Latin class, two members have we given,
Two more are ours, two more have striven.
To battle with the giant, yes, to awaken from its slumber.
Their mind's uncounted riches;
and to gain themselves a place among the learned numbers.

MISS FANNIE HEBR

Prof. Jimmie caused me to criticise my conduct most severely by repeating a couplet relating to a person who scolds. His words fell like wooden weights on my ears, & I hope to profit by them. Not that I scold, but that I may watch my conduct more closely.

Pract. Grammar was some better today. One of my classes in Arith. is doing well, & some pupils in both classes are doing all they can. Others are not. Class in Physiology is deeply interested.

S. T. PEARSON

Wednesday, Oct. 4.
The snap! the snap! O how I love to hear that sound,
When with lessons perfect each is found,
For well it says, in a merry winning tone.
"The fact that I have studied, must be known,"
But, snap, snap, from morn 'til noon, from noon 'til eve.
Asking a drink of water or the room to leave;
Is but the sound of the laggard's wail,
The same, the oft repeated tale.
Surely, there can be no earthly use, in heaping on your teacher
    such abuse.

MISS FANNIE HEBR

I scarce can find a word to say,
Of what has transpired this lovely day,
Yet all have worked with a right good will,
And tried their teaching mandates to fulfill.
These words are simple but the fact do I adore,
For they have done their best, and angels can do no more.

MISS FANNIE HEBR

Two little boys got mad this morning—however, no one was badly hurt and the boys have made up.

This closes the first month's work and the children have done remarkably well and I trust that the remainder of the term will be still more profitably spent. I must add that I am pleased with the work and appreciate the love and kindness shown me by the little boys & girls in my department. I shall remember especially the quantity of flowers.

MISS HATTIE PERRYMAN

Monday, Oct. 9—1893.
Olaf (better known as "Tinkum") Welch joined our noble band again this morning. His number is 126. Pupils inclined to be noisy. Some of my best girls caused me to frown more than once. Too much noise in the house during recesses. Poor lessons with one or two exceptions.

J. M. PEARSON

S. M. Pearson & Marvin McClendon asked permission to quit History.—said they had enough studies without it. Had an interesting lesson.

All of English class failed except Sam Herzfeld. Pract. Grammar class failed. One of the boys in Elocution class had his feelings sticking out too far, and they got hurt. Cooper McClendon says she don't think it makes any difference what sign is put between fractions.

S. G. PEARSON

Am I a felon, that I should such a load of anguish bear?
Is there no one to whom I can of this trouble give a share?
No, dear pen, thou art the only one who I can trust!
This secret thou wilt keep, I know thou wilt, thou must.
Whild stepping lightly through the room
Oh, horrors, what must I see! This was my doom.
A prescription, fresh from the hand of Dr. Charles Adams bold
For Johnnie Ingram—for rat poison—so it the druggist told
His intent so rash, so wild, he did not try to hide,
In words most plain he wrote, "He wants to commit
    siouxeyesighed"!

Miss Fannie Hebr

This is the beginning of a new month. My earnest wish is that teachers and pupils may be inspired with renewed energy and enthusiasm, and I sincerely trust our efforts to succeed in our work may be doubled and that much more may be accomplished this month.

Miss Susie Sutton

Tuesday Oct. 10, 1893.
Some improvement to-day in both lessons and order. Class in Civics debated, "Resolved, that it is right for a man without children to pay school taxes," and as a matter of consolation to this unfortunate creature, I record here that his side (the negative) won the victory. Judging from the earnestness manifested by some of the boys on the Negative, I say there will be more than one old bachelor in the crowd, but I sincerely desire a better state of affairs.

J. M. Pearson

Tuesday Oct. 10, 1893.
From the time when the boys first entered these portals so
    bright,
Their visions have grown deeper and wider,
Till now Charles Adams can see by his might
That to eat goobers in school is not right.

Miss Fannie Hebr

Wednesday, Oct. 11, 1893.
Geometry class had a good lesson. Some of the pupils have not yet learned how to walk, and some have learned how to talk, and I am sorry to say that some have to not know for what school-houses are built. They run they jump, they scream, they hollow, they almost drive me crazy. Eunice Walker entertains me well with her work in Mental Arithmetic, I had to keep her standing near me for two full periods. Chris Young visited us today. I go home tired.

J. M. Pearson

Wednesday, Oct. 11, 1893.
Miss Eunice Walker
Is quite a candid talker.
With gestures profuse in a manner most gay,
These are the words, which I by chance, heard her say;
"Dear Clara, do you not find Latin a terrible bore?
To me of horrors, it sho' am one more,
That old Caesar *to-lose*, I am not one bit too good,
But she would not *believe* me even if I should." Now Eunice,
  my child,
Why this tirade, so wild,
Pray your good senses retain,
And remember, that you alone, suffer the loss or reap the sole
  gain.
                                              MISS FANNIE HEBR

Thursday, Oct. 12, 1893
  As are the teachers, so are the pupils. If the teacher is dull and
inattentive to his duties, the pupils will soon become so. If the teacher
is wide awake and full of energy, pupils will sooner or later catch the
same disease. *Wouldn't you like to catch it!* Some of us have not yet
learned what it is to be prompt and punctual. Several cases of tardi-
ness, but we have had good lessons to-day.
                                              J. M. PEARSON

In playing so wildly,
Was Cowles badly maimed,
Not halt and blinded, but simply bruised and lamed.
This demanded prohibition, much against my will
I enforced prohibition, from running madly down the hill.
                                              MISS FANNIE HEBR

Friday, Oct. 13, 1893.
  Religious exercises conducted by Bro. Brewer. Weather cloudy and
cold. Had to have fires made in all the rooms. Class in Civics debated,
"Resolved, That it is right for women to vote in municipal elections."
  S. G. Pearson and Miss Sutton decided the question in favor of the
negative. Willie Vernon's speech put him forever on record as a lady's
man.   J. M. PEARSON

  We begin the day's work with a good class in History by all the class.
The lessons have all been good & interesting. But it is strange and
amusing to see how *hard* some boys will try to talk & do things without
the teacher's knowing it. They will even try to pass goobers during a
recitation. We close with a debate in which the boys acquitted themselves manfully, and all go home with our hearts full of happiness.
                                              S. G. PEARSON

Monday, Oct. 16—1893.
Willie Pearson, our little captain, our little gabber,
Who keeps up with Willie Stearns, such an incessant jabber,
Is sick to-day but bless his little heart,
We each one hope that he'll soon be back and begin in silence
      to do his part.

Miss Fannie Hebr

The little girls have decided that it isn't necessary to drink water so
often and order has reigned to-day. With only a few exceptions, the
noblest desires have manifested themselves in the children. We *labor*
to implant a truth in the child-mind, and it is *sad* to see the labor lost.

S. G. Pearson

We had a "Knotty" question given by Prof. Jimmie in squares and
angles. Most of the lessons have been good to-day. Some of the boys
still think it is their duty to talk at recitations. And for this offense a
place that is wide and vacant *may* be allotted to the offender ere
another week passes. Order *must* reign, or teaching will be a failure.

S. G. Pearson

Friday, Oct. 20—1893.
Bible reading and prayer by Bro. McCoy. We are always glad to have
the Preachers visit us. Class in Civics debated, "Resolved, That the
mental capacities of the male sex are superior to those of the Female".
Although the boys on the Aff. made splendid speeches, they failed to
make the Pres. think they were right.

J. M. Pearson

Evolution is not relegated to the past.
Conclusive proof of this I've found at last.
Willie Pearson, once thought to be quite sage.
Kicks at the girls, just like a mule, in this declining age.

Miss Fannie Hebr

Our two little Willie's had the practice begun
Of grasping their hats before the bell had rung.
When told that this was far from right
They'd hide them near, just out of sight.
When this their teacher them denied,
They boldly yet her rule defied. When they received for this
      the gift of store,
It did appear as though they'd disobey no more.

Miss Fannie Hebr

Surely some good has been accomplished to-day, some good impres-
sion made, for the children want to be good—What do I say? They *want*

to be good! Surely they do! Else, why this striving to excel.—Why, this eagerness to recite a lesson,—Why this desire to tell what they know? No! I do not, I *can* not mistake when I say these dear girls and boys *are* good children.

S. G. PEARSON

[The following Diary of a few days by Miss Sutton was not handed in in time, and could not be recorded in regular order.]

Tuesday, Oct. 17.
The privileges of teachers were kindly enumerated by the pupils in general exercises. I am pleased to record that ice-cream, potatoes and jam were among the good things which they thought we might enjoy.

Thursday, Oct. 19.
The lessons to-day were unusually good. The girls are very much excited over the Concert Christmas. Day after day, I hear the question, "What will I play at the Concert?"

Friday, Oct. 20.
Truly it is sweet to be remembered. Who can say that a teacher's work is hard when there is so much to make us enjoy it? I was the recipient of some pretty flowers and lots of good things. I was even presented with a rat—it was a candy one though. That is the only kind I am fond of, children.

Tuesday, Oct. 23.
One of my girls, Dora Thomas, had a painful accident this afternoon, which will deprive us of her bright presence for awhile. She sprained her ankle playing "Crazy Liza", and she decided that she won't indulge in crazy games any more.

Thursday, Oct. 25.
All seemed particularly gay and festive this morning. We had more singing than usual, Every body sang "Tra-la-la" and "Sweet Summer's Gone Away" and seemed to be more familiar with them than with the Lord's Prayer, which was the closing chant.

Friday, Oct. 26.
I have had good lessons today, I paid a pleasant visit to the primary room this morning and can testify that one lesson at least, was good and the department excellent; but that goes without saying,—with such a skillful directress at the head. I charge fifty cents for that, Miss Hattie.

You know there is a music teacher here who has a weakness for bananas, candy etc.

The debate this afternoon was fine. The number of points used and the depth of the arguments was bewildering to we three, poor judges, but boys! I heard that the girls said that some of you attracted them more than your speeches did, one young gentleman especially was the admired of the admired. I refer to the one with the new suit of clothes. He is intimately connected with the Brewery. I gained a nice new pupil, but sad to relate—the bird has flown.

It was the handsome brother of one of the teachers. Ah well! I hold that "it is better to have gained and lost than never to have gained at all."

MISS SUSIE SUTTON

Monday Oct. 30—1893

Pupils have done much better to-day than they did last Monday. Heard Miss Perryman's class in History recite a part of their lesson. The work was interesting. A visit to the little folks' department always encourages me. I love the children. They are full of life. They teach me something. Teachers can not afford to get old in their ways.

J. M. PEARSON

The new week's work has opened up with a number of sick pupils returned, and all seem ready & willing to work. Chrysanthemums in profusion are brought to me each day. The lessons in my department have been well prepared.

MISS HATTIE PERRYMAN

> The Council kindly came and listened to the diary, or rather
> the reading of the same.
> Someone said after the records had been read,
> That I recorded mostly bad things and left the good unsaid.
> There is a time for flattery and for praising,
> A time for souls in music raising.
> But the good things are so numerous, that for them we have no
> room.
> So to reap the tears which you have sown will be your doom.
> If I the various bad things did reject,
> My diary might present a very monotonous effect.

MISS FANNIE HEBR

Exercises opened by reading the diary. The City Council was present and visited the little folks room before leaving. They said many encouraging things, and the day seems brighter and we feel that their visit did good; although they did not hear any of the recitations. The watchword given in the morning was very good. "He who attends to his own business has a good steady employment."

MISS HATTIE PERRYMAN

Robbie Little says "Georgie" Washington was at the head of the first American army. My little folks are doing some lovely work in both Geography and History. The maps of South America are especially good.

MISS HATTIE PERRYMAN

Lessons very good. A great deal of interest is being manifested by my pupils, I am glad to say they seem interested especially in History & Geography. One little boy said the American Army was very "blue," he meant they were not trained, rather green about fighting in battles.

Miss Hattie Perryman

Right has surely conquered to-day. And it may be the *watchword* of this morning caused a closer inspection into our evil natures, and brought in light that cloud of selfishness that has so long shut out the bright sunlight of happiness. How gladly would we confess a fault that robs us of happiness. A closely contested spelling match reveals the fact that the little girls are happy; and we go home willing to confess our faults, and grow wiser & better.

S. G. Pearson

Lessons have been good all day. In the afternoon we had regular lessons until recess—After recess the little girls recited some pieces. The larger boys and girls tried to see who could get mention in the diary by giving the greatest number of trees, flowers or birds. Vessie Calvin gave the names of eighteen birds. The children have done satisfactory work this week.

Miss Hattie Perryman

Monday, Nov. 6,—1893.
Last week we had Ham but no Polk. To-day we have no Ham. What will we do? We have only one Glass for the whole room; our Lake is absent; the Brewer(y) is not represented; and we haven't a single Christian. Willie Darsey is absent, but we still have a King and Pearsons four, a Wilder pair and Moore. Excellent work for Monday.

J. M. Pearson

School opened this morning very encouragingly. I had forty bright, beaming faces in my room, and had some good work done. All the children in the Primary department are not angels, but when they do their best we have some good lessons and try to forget the little naughty, bad traits.

Miss Hattie Perryman

Of doing nothing the two little Willies became quite tired,
In studying they do not believe;
These are boys who can neither be persuaded nor hired.
But at last, they were led by a kind and loving fate,
They would see, who of the two could the funniest tale relate.
Willie Stearns was the champion, he was the Knight,
His tale was so funny that the other Willie tittered outright.

Miss Fannie Hebr

The day is dark but not gloomy; for who could be otherwise than merry with so many smiling sweet, little faces? They bring any amount of pretty flowers, and so many treats in the way of candies, cane, grapes, apples, and other good things. A teacher in the Primary room doesn't have such a hard life after all. "Every sweet has its bitter," of course, "as every violet hath its grave."

Miss Hattie Perryman

Wednesday, Nov. 8—1893.

Geometry class is again in trouble. Class in English Grammar could do better. Other classes did well to-day. Class in Civics debated, Resolved, That it is wrong for teachers to inflict corporal punishment in the presence of the school. The Affirmative won, thought the negative made some strong arguments in favor of preserving that custom of antiquity.

J. M. Pearson

My room has been lively to-day. Forty little voices have said *"Miss Perryman"* ever so many times and if the lesson was very good, three or four wanted to ask questions at once. Prof. Pearson visited the little band and they all felt privileged to ask him some questions. My little classes are developing wonderfully fast. Our pet boy, Leon Nolen, has been teaching some new tricks to those not so wise. He runs Lesis Coley very much, to-day she is sick. Willie Barton is the finest flower girl I know.

Miss Hattie Perryman

Friday, Nov. 10—1893.

Work *in school-room* has been pleasant and all have made some progress. Outside interference has given me no little trouble, but

"Trouble never stop forever,
The darkest day will pass away."
"The oak grows stronger
By the winds that toss its branches."
"Hope may be drenched, but it can not be drowned."

J. M. Pearson

This has been a busy day. The work has been very satisfactory. Some little disturbance among the little girls, but they are all as good or better friends than ever. I am glad to say my crowd of little folks are getting on beautifully.

Miss Hattie Perryman

We have a new pupil in our room this morning, and all seems bright enough; but outside it is a cold and rainy,—One of Longfellow's perfect Nov. days.

MISS FANNIE HEBR

Wednesday, Nov. 15, 1893.

Winter is on us this morning. Good fires are in demand and Marvin & Jack are over ready to bring in wood and coal. We are doing as well as could be expected with neither a Doctor nor a Christian Present.

J. M. PEARSON

(Wednesday, Nov. 15, 1893.)

Classes have done remarkably well. Vivian gave me a cold reception this morning. She threw her arms around my neck and left a great piece of ice on my collar.

MISS HATTIE PERRYMAN

Friday, Nov. 17—93.

The good work continues. This has been our best week. Our only complaint is that some have been tardy at opening. Class in Civics debated, "Resolved, That the Pulpit affords a greater field for eloquence than the Bar." Both sides did well but the Affirmative won. We go home feeling that we have done good work this week.

J. M. PEARSON

The work has been so pleasant to-day that I go home really feeling glad I am a teacher. The work for the entire week has been good and I have nothing to worry over. Clyde and Sidney have been extra smart with their reading lessons this week.

MISS HATTIE PERRYMAN

Tuesday, Nov. 21

To acquire a pure, strong character is the grandest work of man. We are building every day. Let us lay a solid foundation. Boys and girls, for your sake, for my sake, for the sake of your families, for the sake of future usefulness, for eternity's sake, do your own thinking; don't copy the work of another's brain, shake off your laziness, ask no favors, don't whine, strive to do God's will.

J. M. PEARSON

I have had a jolly little crowd of forty three to-day, and we have done some good work. Robbie Little & Ray Nolin, seem to think whistling essential to thorough instruction. I suppose I will be like a writer once I read of, who thought heaven would not be complete without a boy whistling there.

Some bad fairies have visited Roy Wilder to-day, and he has given us the other side of his disposition.

MISS HATTIE PERRYMAN

The work in this room has been very good to-day. Every one seemed musically inclined this morning. Miss Hebr added much to the singing by giving her help——to hold the book.

Miss Hattie Perryman

Weather has been cool and cloudy. Children have spent as much time as possible around the fires, but have done good work. Mental Arithmetic class is in trouble. Grammar class is improving. Brag Algebra class holds its own.

J. M. Pearson

"All is quiet on the Potomac." The day has passed pleasantly. Lessons have been good and order reasonably so. The children are living in hopes that Santa Claus will soon drive around and let the holidays begin.

Miss Hattie Perryman

Friday, Nov. 24.
Class in Civics debated, Resolved, That there should be an education qualification for suffrage. This proved to be an interesting subject. Some good speeches were made on both sides, but the affirmative won.

J. M. Pearson

Thursday, Nov. 16.
I suppose it won't do to praise too much, and I certainly am not given to flattery, but I know that I have the best and sweetest set of girls (and boys too, for that matter,) to be found anywhere. Did they know how glad I am to see their interest and what encouragement it gives me, I am sure they would keep it up.

Miss Susie Sutton

Friday, Nov. 24.
I have had so many flowers, fruits and good things to-day and every body has been so nice to me that I am in good humor with all the world. The moral is to keep bringing me good things, girls.

Miss Susie Sutton

Katie and Blanche and Albert and Sammie
P. Y. and Otho and Emmett and Annie,
    The model Arithmetic class
Came up with a lesson that would not pass.
    Although they declared, their task they did not shirk.
Yet not one problem did they work.
    They were fearless in honesty, but their hearts with sorrow
        did ache.
As it beat in sympathy for their dear grade's sake.

Miss Fannie Hebr

The day is cold, so cold; but in my room it is so very comfortable that I hardly realize the wind is blowing—The children have enjoyed the day I think. I have extracted two teeth to-day. I believe that makes about eleven in all. Van can't make a wry face but once a day it seems.

Thus ends the week's work and we all go home to good fires and plenty of quiet.

MISS HATTIE PERRYMAN

In English little Ellis Floyd
Was well overjoyed;
We answered each question with an air of—don't—
bother—me. I can-not-think.
That he gained his point, he showed by a ludicrous wink.
When he began at Bennie to wink,
I began to think
(As his heart, from its exalted mirthful seat
Broke asunder and settled to the soles of his feet)
That it made of him a better boy
That with his teacher's patience he must not toy.

MISS FANNIE HEBR

The rain was just coming down in torrents this morning, but quite a number of us got over here and went to work as if the skies were clear.

MISS HATTIE PERRYMAN

Wednesday, Nov. 29.
Some of the pupils have had too much frolic on the brain all day. Chas. Brewer, Oliver Posey, Olney Goggans, and Joe Archer made a complete failure in the debate. A visit to the Primary room was necessary to revive my spirits after these failures. Work has not been satisfactory throughout the day.

J. M. PEARSON

The little girls have done all they could to prepare their lessons well. They have studied with earnestness, and have asked several times if we were going to observe Thanksgiving day.

But a definite answer could not be given to this question till the hour for dismission.

After the Diary was read, we received the news that we might rest tomorrow, and join the people of this nation in ascribing praise to "Him from whom all blessings flow."

S. G. PEARSON

In Caesar Annie C. read her lesson so fast.
That the others to her could a shadow not cast.
The reading was lovely—her translation most fluent and free.
But of so many words what could the constructions be?

This was a very foolish question to ask one who could Latin
   read so well;
Answers to such questions she did not deign to tell.
But simply referred us to "The Ark" where is found
Notes on such questions, by the pound.

MISS FANNIE HEBR

Tuesday, Dec. 5, 1893.
A King with one good arm is better than no King, so we gladly
welcome Basil back this morning. We are also glad to have Mattie
More with us again, after an absence of two days. We regret that
Marvin McClendon has gone into the "Dago" business and will not be
with us again until after Christmas. We all miss Marvin. Pupils have
done good work to-day.

J. M. PEARSON

Some of the boys think they should have the privilege of looking in
their books, although they try to conceal it. I will not give their names,
for I hope they will leave off this sly way of acting.

S. G. PEARSON

We rejoice to-day for one of our lost jewels has been found;
Little Sam is given back—quite well and sound.

MISS FANNIE HEBR

Wednesday, Dec. 6.
Ada Street is in her place again. She was absent Monday & Tuesday.
Class in Civics debates, Resolved, "That Washington deserves greater
praise for defending than Columbus for discovering America." Deci-
sion was rendered in favor of affirmative. Grammar class is improving.
Mental Arithmetic classes dull. Algebra classes not up to the standard.
I had to rebuke an evil spirit that entered into some of the boys.

J. M. PEARSON

Chas. Brewer, although he is late, each morning to his Latin
   class comes down
With a smile and not a frown;
He is not late because his lesson he does not know;
For if it were thus, he would not be smiling so.
In this he had a motive—so he said—
But maybe it's because he has a Christian in his hand.

MISS FANNIE HEBR

"Well begun is half done." My little folks worked beautifully in the
forenoon, but seemed a little inclined to idle the rest of the day. But all
things come to those who wait and work earnestly.
So to-morrow will probably end a more satisfactory day's work.

MISS HATTIE PERRYMAN

Thursday, Dec. 7.

Dora Thomas paid us a visit this morning. The diagram system has put new life into my Grammar class. Class in Civics seemed to enjoy their recitation but they didn't know much about this lesson. I give a few of their answers; "Alabama has three U.S. Senators," "The Governor is elected every six years," "The Legislature meets twice a year," & etc. It is nothing but right for me to say that Willie Dorsey never makes such mistakes.

J. M. PEARSON

Thursday, Dec. 7—1893.

It is work from day to day, and duty after duty comes crowding upon us, bidding us to be faithful, and pointing to the chaplet of intellectual beauty that none but the diligent can wear, inspires us with brighter visions of those altitudes of thoughts that lift us up and fill us with greater desires to reach after those attractions that draw us upward.

Some of my girls are working so well I had to tell Prof. Jimmy about it. And if they will continue to do well, I'm going to tell the whole school of their diligence. They are working with a will.

S. G. PEARSON

Friday, Dec. 8.

Pupils have done good work today. Class in Civics proved that. "The pen is mightier than the sword," My boys will be ready in a short while to attempt "to speak in public on the stage."

J. M. PEARSON

Friday, Dec. 8—1893.

The little girls were so anxious for a spelling-match this afternoon, I thought at one time I'd have to yield. We get out a little earlier, and are glad 'tis Friday.

S. G. PEARSON

As nothing of importance has occurred,
My notes of length will be deferred.
MISS FANNIE HEBR

Tuesday, Dec. 12, 1894.

Our Class is with us to-day. This has not been our best day. Class in Civics failed again. Some of the boys evidently don't read much.

J. M. PEARSON

To-day like yesterday, in lack of comment, is the same,
On the boys so good, must fall the blame.
MISS FANNIE HEBR

Dec. 13.

Some of the pupils are still absent. Colds are raging and children are coughing.

Debating class proved that freedom has benefitted the negro race. Children have not done their best.

J. M. PEARSON

To-day has been pleasant enough as to the work the children have done, but O, *how Sick* I am! This afternoon I called on Sallie May Adams, P. Y. Willis and Charles Pearson to relieve me, which they did cheerfully, and I must say they did remarkably well as little teachers. I go home with a burning fever and full of pain.

S. G. PEARSON

Will wonders never cease?
Will always reign this quiet peace?
MISS FANNIE HEBR

Friday, Dec. 15—1894.

Our sick list is growing. I hope all will be well next week. Our debating class had quite a lively time discussing the merits of the ox and the mule, and as usual, the ox came out winner. Children were too much disposed to frolic to-day.

J. M. PEARSON

This week, forget, I could not, if I would
The boys have been so very, very good.
MISS FANNIE HEBR

Studies of Folk Play
And Folk Say

Some scholars have begun to use the term childlore as a designation for those segments of folklore that, either by practice or tradition, are associated with the child: riddles, nonsense verse, games, taunts, parodies, tongue-twisters, and jump-rope rhymes. While childlore may be useful as a classifying term, strictly speaking, there is no "folklore for children" in the same sense as there is a special literature for children. Folk tales still have wide currency in publications for younger readers, but these are usually literary retellings of world folk narratives, and the American folk heroes of cartoons and movies, like Johnny Appleseed, Paul Bunyan, and Ichabod Crane, were, from the beginning, literary creations. Duncan Emrich, almost alone among folklore scholars, has collected and presented childlore in a format attractive to older children (see *The Nonsense Book of Riddles, Rhymes, Tongue-Twisters, Puzzles, and Jokes from American Folklore*, New York: Four Winds Press, 1970, and *The Hodge-Podge Book, An Almanac of American Folklore*, Four Winds Press, 1972). Emrich's *The Whim-Wham Book* (New York: Four Winds Press, 1975) is almost entirely a collection of folklore now current among schoolchildren. His books are all handsomely printed, with spirited illustrations by Ib Ohlsson. The scholar will be pleased with the extensive bibliographical references.

Children do indeed deserve printed collections of folklore, but it is only fair to remind ourselves that oral folk traditions have always been shared by children and their elders, that folklore is transmitted from adult to child as well as from child to child. Certainly some songs, tales, rhymes, and games flourish with the child, who assimilates folklore, from whatever source, naturally and unconsciously, but these are all taught and nurtured by the old as well as by youthful contemporaries. Our Alabama informants were fairly evenly divided between adults and children, and the findings of the Troy State University student collectors argue strongly against a lore that belongs exclusively to the child. The spirit of the folklore in *Zickary Zan*, derived as it is from informants of all ages, is, however, childlike, at once merry and innocent, sad and wise.

That spirit illuminates the work of William W. Newell, who made the earliest important study of children's games in America, *Games and Songs of American Children* (New York: Harper and Brothers, 1883; revised 1903; reprinted Dover, 1963). One of the founders of the American Folklore Society and editor of *The Journal of American Folklore*, Newell was interested in such diverse matters as Arthurian legends, Child ballads, and the lore of the American Negro and Indian. Including material from New England to the Middle

Atlantic states and as far south as Georgia, his collection represents the first attempt at the systematic classification of children's games in this country. His methodology became standard-description, inclusion of song verses, musical notation, dialogue, and chants, the citation of sources and variants, and comparison with the antecedent games of western Europe and England. In the first half of the twentieth century Benjamin Botkin would rely heavily on Newell for his exhaustive survey and study *The American Play Party Song* (reprint, New York: Frederick Ungar, 1963). Newell was interested in the descent of American folk games from both the ballad and European and English dance, and his classifications range from pantomimes, dances, and courtship games to rhymed verbal pranks and games played with a ball.

Between the first publication of *Games and Songs of American Children* in 1883 and the revised edition of 1903 came an encyclopedic collection of British children's games, *The Traditional Games of England, Scotland, and Ireland*, published in two volumes, 1894 and 1898 (Dover reprint, 1964) by Lady Alice Gomme, who was primarily interested in children's play as a survival of the culture and mythology of primitive man. The Gomme collection reinforced Newell's conclusions about the transmission of British games into the American colonies, and he shared her interest in the mythological aspects of children's games.

Newell was a gifted, charming writer; his accounts are pleasant and highly readable, and the joy of childhood shines on every page. Yet he was wrong on one count—he yearned over the passing of the old games into oblivion. They have certainly not disappeared in Alabama, where they are still enjoyed, nearly a hundred years after his study was first published. Ruby Pickens Tartt and other WPA field workers collected many games in this state during the

1930s; Byron Arnold gathered some in the 1940s for his *Folk Songs of Alabama* (University, Alabama: University of Alabama Press, 1950); Harold Courlander was collecting children's game songs in Sumter County during the late 1950s for a series of recordings issued by Ethnic Folkways; and *Zickary Zan* contains a substantial body of folk games not only retained within the memory of living informants but also played and sung to this day in Alabama schoolyards. Twenty-nine of the folk games in *Zickary Zan* appear in Newell's collection, and that figure, in view of the lapse of a century, is impressive.

Early scholars and collectors, following Newell's lead, were interested in the verbal and musical aspects of games, rhymes, and chants. Now, however, scholars construct models of social and psychological behavior as it emerges from children's games. A definitive study and manual of games is that of Elliot M. Avedon and Brian Sutton-Smith, *The Study of Games* (New York: John Wiley and Sons, 1971). The editors-authors provide extensive comment and bibliography on the history of games, and their functions, procedures, and rules. For a discussion of English games, see Norman Douglas, *London Street Games* (Detroit: Singing Tree Press, 1968, a reissue of an English work by Chatto and Windus, 1931); *The Games of Children: Their Origin and History* (Detroit: Singing Tree Press, 1969, a reissue of an English work published in 1929); and *Children's Singing Games, With the Tunes to Which They are Sung* (New York: Dover Publications, 1967, reissue of an 1894 English work by David Nutt). Kate Greenaway fans will be delighted with the reissue of her *Book of Games*, first published in 1889, by Viking Press (New York, 1976), which describes seventy-seven pleasant diversions ranging from kites and soap bubbles to tag and word games. The illustrations are numerous and fine.

Jump-rope rhymes, widely collected all over America, are among the largest categories of childlore. They appear in WPA folk archives, in results of limited field collections from New Rochelle to Los Angeles, in university archives and collections, in various folklore quarterlies, in published collections of verbal folklore such as the volumes by Emrich, and in other general published collections and anthologies of nonsense verse, jingles, chants, riddles, proverbs, and the like. The broadest study is by Roger D. Abrahams, *Jump Rope Rhymes: A Dictionary* (Austin: The University of Texas Press, 1969), which lists the appearance of 619 rhymes in various printed collections, with an introduction on jump games.

Counting-out rhymes and taunts have received critical attention, both in bibliography and analysis, and isolated studies and collections turn up in folklore quarterlies and in anthologies such as B. A. Botkin's *A Treasury of American Folklore* (New York, 1944). The standard reference in counting-out rhymes was first issued in 1888: Henry Carrington Boulton, *The Counting-Out Rhymes of Children, Their Antiquity, Origin, and Wide Distribution*, which contained 877 rhymes grouped by countries. Boulton's work has been reprinted by Singing Tree Press, Detroit, 1969. Taunts are usually included in collections of nonsense verse and miscellanies. There are two recent studies: Ray B. Browne, "Children's Taunts, Teases, and Disrespectful Sayings From Southern California," *Western Folklore* 13 (1954), 190–198 and "Children's Taunts, Teases, etc. from Alabama," *Western Folklore* 14 (1955), 206–207.

Riddles rank with jump-rope rhymes in collection, critical study, and bibliography; Archer Taylor's *English Riddles from Oral Tradition* (University of

California Press, 1951) is the definitive text; (see also Carol Withers and Sula Benet, *The American Riddle Book*, New York, 1954, and various articles on riddles by Archer Taylor in folklore quarterlies as cited in *Social Sciences and Humanities Index*). Vance Randolph, the great Ozark folklorist, has also collected riddles; see, for example, Vance Randolph and Archer Taylor, "Riddles in the Ozarks," *Southern Folklore Quarterly* 8 (1944), 1–10.

The full history of autograph albums is, so far as we can tell, yet to be written. Entire albums, such as the two in *Zickary Zan*, are frequently uncovered and published; and often an investigator will study the autograph verse and emblems of contemporary schoolchildren. Alan Dundes in "Some Examples of Infrequently Reported Autograph Verse" (*Southern Folklore Quarterly*, vol. 26, 1962, 127–130) and W. K. McNeil in "The Autograph Album Custom: A Tradition and its Scholarly Treatment" (*Keystone Folklore Quarterly*, vol. 13, Spring 1968, 29–40) have laid the foundations for an extended study of this particular kind of folk verse.

Nonsense or fun verse does not really exist as a distinct classification, but rather as a marked characteristic of jump-rope and counting-out rhymes, taunts, and autograph verse. Nonsense stanzas often migrate to folk songs, and vice versa; a sung nonsense rhyme may become a part of oral humor, or the rhyme may exist as both song and recitation. Nonsense is firmly established in Anglo-American folk tradition, not only in verbal lore but also in actual practice—contests in which the participants are frogs, turtles, and earthworms, mock-solemn ceremonies on Ground-hog Day, college stunt nights where parody mingles with nonsense, and such television programs as "Truth or Consequences," "Almost Anything Goes," and "Sesame Street," which is certainly the most charming nonsense-sense of a television century. Generally, nonsense stanzas are tossed into miscellanies of folk rhymes like those of Emrich or into anthologies of folklore, although small separate collections sometimes turn up in periodicals.

The standard reference for proverbs is by Archer Taylor and Bartlett Jere Whiting, *Dictionary of American Proverbs and Proverbial Phrases, 1820–1880* (Cambridge, Massachusetts: Harvard University Press, 1958), and the chief study is Taylor's *The Proverb* (Cambridge: Harvard University Press, 1931, reissued by Hatboro in 1962).

Two British couples have established themselves as the most prominent scholars and collectors in Anglo-American nursery rhymes, a great body of verse, both printed and oral, which includes folk games, taunts, riddles, songs, chants, parodies, and nonsense. Iona and Peter Opie have edited three major volumes: *The Oxford Dictionary of Nursery Rhymes* (New York: Oxford University Press, 1951), *The Oxford Nursery Rhyme Book* (New York: Oxford University Press, 1960), and *The Lore and Language of School Children* (New York: Oxford University Press, 1959). The Baring-Goulds, William S. and Cecil, have edited *The Annotated Mother Goose* (New York: Clarkson N. Potter, 1962), the first ten chapters of which are arranged according to major printed collections of nursery rhymes. The last half of the Baring-Gould collection consists of nursery rhymes associated with seasons, weather, charms, and nature; lullabies and game songs, riddles and tongue twisters; proverbs, nineteenth-century collections or "bonquets," and twentieth-century Mother Goose verse.

The book itself is most attractive, the illustrations are reproductions of famous originals, and the notes to each rhyme are excellent.

Anthologies of American folklore that contain representative collections of jump-rope rhymes, games, counting-out rhymes, nonsense verse and parodies, riddles, taunts, autograph-album verse, and proverbs, such as the Botkin and Emrich series, are listed in the bibliographical section of *Cracklin Bread and Asfidity*. The reader is also directed to the bibliographical issues of the *Southern Folklore Quarterly* under the appropriate divisions, for articles that present studies and collections of these folklore categories. The most useful bibliographies in American folklore are those which appear in major full-length critical studies and collections: Richard Dorson's *American Folklore* (University of Chicago Press, 1959), to which is appended a bibliographical essay for every chapter; the works of Duncan Emrich, especially *Folklore on the American Land* (Boston: Little, Brown, and Company, 1974); Jan Harold Brunvand's *The Study of American Folklore: An Introduction* (New York, 1968); and Tristram P. Coffin's (ed.) *Our Living Traditions: An Introduction to American Folklore* (New York, 1968). The first volume of the outstanding regional folklore survey, *The Frank C. Brown Collection of Folklore* (Durham: The University of North Carolina Press, 7 vols., 1952–1964), is devoted to folk games and verbal lore, with games edited by Paul Brewster, riddles by Archer Taylor, and proverbs by Bartlett Jere Whiting.

Scholarship in the folklore of Alabama deserves special mention. The Library of Congress holds one annotated bibliography of Alabama folklore, a manuscript of forty typewritten pages dated January 12, 1969, compiled by Cary R. Smith apparently when he was a graduate student at Indiana University. Smith cites both full-length studies and articles appearing in periodicals, and the serious student of Alabama folklore will want to obtain a copy of his bibliography. His assertion that "there has been little accurate and serious scholarship in the state" is largely correct but calls for qualification and explanation, especially in view of the fact that a decade has gone by since Smith conducted his survey. Additionally, the Smith bibliography does not cite those collections made by field workers of the WPA National Writer's Project, Folklore Division, in Alabama during the 1930s. These field studies are far from negligible—Alabama's WPA folk-song collection ranks with the finest in the entire nation, especially that outstanding body of Negro religious and secular songs collected by Ruby Pickens Tartt in Sumter County; the Alabama *Slave Narratives* are measurably richer in folk-life profiles than are most of the *Narratives* from other states; and the folk tales, although scant and not representative of the entire state, are diverse and interesting. The manuscripts of the WPA folklore collections are on deposit at the Alabama State Department of Archives and History in Montgomery and the Library of Congress; the Alabama *Slave Narratives*, both those deposited in Montgomery and at the Library of Congress, have been edited, along with the *Narratives* from other states by George P. Rawick in the monumental *The American Slave: A Composite Autobiography* (Westport, Connecticut: Greenwood Press, 1977). Nineteen volumes appeared in 1972 and 1973, sixteen volumes of *Narratives* exactly as they were submitted by the various states to the Washington office, two volumes of slave interviews conducted prior to the WPA project at Fisk Univer-

sity, and Rawick's treatise on slavery. In 1977 Rawick published twelve supplemental volumes of *Narratives* that had been scattered in various libraries
throughout the country. The Alabama *Narratives* appear in volume six of series
one and volume one of the supplemental volumes.

Since 1950 Alabama can lay claim to a prominent American folklore scholar
and collector, Professor Ray B. Browne, now head of the Center for Popular
Culture at Bowling Green State University, Bowling Green, Ohio, and editor of
The Journal of Popular Culture. Professor Browne has published numerous
articles in which he reported his findings in Alabama taunts and teases,
nonsense orations, and folk tales. His Ph.D. dissertation, filed at the Library of
Congress, was a handsome collection of folk songs primarily from Randolph
County; his monograph *Popular Beliefs and Practices from Alabama* (Berkeley
and Los Angeles: The University of California Press, 1958, Folklore Studies 9) is
a first-rate, full survey of Alabama superstitions, remedies, and traditional
beliefs; and his most recent publication *A Night with the "Hants"* (Bowling
Green, Popular Press, Bowling Green University, 1976) broke new ground in
the methodology, philosophy, and presentation of folk tales. The Alabama
Council on the Arts and Humanities has recently appointed a coordinator of
folklore, Hank Willet, whose articles on Alabama folklore and folk life are
printed in newspapers throughout the state. Elaine Katz, who teaches an
introductory folklore course at The University of Alabama, has recently published her lively book *Folklore: For the Time of Your Life* (Birmingham, Alabama: Oxmoor House, 1978), which offers practical advice to the amateur
collector and which touches on several important aspects of Alabama's folk
life and traditions.

As Smith suggests, much of Alabama folklore and folk life is embedded in
early histories, literary sources, private diaries and memoirs, and local histories. Among the most important of the literary sources are the Simon Suggs
stories and local-color sketches of James Johnson Hooper and Joseph G.
Baldwin's *Flush Times of Mississippi and Alabama*, first published in 1833. The
definitive biography of Hooper, *Alias Simon Suggs* (University of Alabama
Press, 1952), was written by another Alabamian, Dr. W. S. Hoole. Early regional and state histories that offer glimpses of Alabama folk life would
include F. L. Olmsted's *A Journey in the Seaboard Slave States* (1859), Thomas S.
Woodward's *Reminiscences of the Creek and Muscogee Indians* (1859), W. H.
Milburn's *The Pioneers, Preachers, and People of the Mississippi Valley* (1860),
the Pickett *History of Alabama* (1896), and A. B. Moore's *History of Alabama*
(1927). Nearly every county and many towns in Alabama possess at least one
written history, but, unfortunately many of the early local histories are not
widely available. A very few histories were prepared for the 1976 Bicentennial
Celebration, for example, *The History of Tallapoosa County* (Alexander City,
Alabama, 1976), a valuable guide to early settlements, schools, and churches of
that area. Alabama deserves a series of county histories, and reprinting the
older local studies would be useful to students of both Alabama folklore and
Alabama history. Alabama folk-life studies often appear in both *The Alabama
Review* and *The Alabama Historical Quarterly*, for example: Hamner Cobbs'
series on Negro humor, speech, and superstitions (*Alabama Review*, vol. 5,
1952, 203–212; vol. 11, 1958, 55–56; vol. 17, 1964, 163–180), Eugene Current-

Garcia's "Newspaper Humor in the Old South, 1835–1855" (*Alabama Review*, vol. 2, 1949, 102–121), and a companion piece on political jokes by his Auburn University colleague Robert Partin, "Alabama Newspaper Humor During Reconstruction" (*Alabama Review*, vol. 17, 1964, 243–260), two articles by Laura F. Murphy on Alabama Cajuns (*Alabama Historical Quarterly*, vol. 1, 1930, 77–86, vol. 2, 1940, 416–427), and a study of Black Belt funeral customs by Renwick C. Kennedy, "Alas, Poor Yorick" (*Alabama Historical Quarterly*, vol. 21, 1940, 405–415). Personal papers, letters, and diaries are often excellent sources for folk-life studies; several full-length publications exist, including Virginia Clay-Clopton's *A Belle of the Fifties* (New York: Doubleday, 1905), Anne Hobson's *In Old Alabama* (New York: Doubleday, 1903), and Anne Royall's *Letters from Alabama* (privately printed in Washington, D.C., 1830, now available in a new edition with introduction).

In addition to Professor Brown's researches, there are several other notable, extensive efforts in Alabama folklore—Carl Carmer's pioneer work *Stars Fell on Alabama* (New York: Farrar and Rinehart, 1934), Julian Lee Rayford's collection of tales and legends from the Mobile Bay and Dauphin Island, *Whistlin' Woman and Crowin' Hen* (Mobile: Rankin Press, 1956), the important volume *Folksongs of Alabama* (University of Alabama Press, 1950) by Byron Arnold, and a new book about place names in Sumter County, Alabama, by Dr. Virginia Foscue (University of Alabama Press, 1979). There are two remarkably fine disc anthologies of field recordings made in Alabama by Harold Courlander, *Negro Folk Music of Alabama* (Ethnic Folkways, FE 4417, 4418, 4471, 4472, 4473, 4474), and by Frederick J. Ramsey, *Music from the South* (ten volumes, Ethnic Folkways, FA 2650–2659). John Lomax recorded hundreds of folk songs in Alabama for the Library of Congress in 1934, 1937, and 1939; duplicates of these recordings may be obtained from the Library of Congress where they are deposited. Lou Ellen Ballard's unpublished thesis, "Folktales from Spring Hill, Pigeon Creek, and Happy Hollow. A Study of Alabama Folk Tales," is filed at the Ralph Draughon Library, Auburn University.

Our survey of *The Journal of American Folklore* and the *Southern Folklore Quarterly* turned up a surprising amount of Alabama folklore scholarship, which the following brief bibliography will indicate:

Ballard, Lou Ellen. "Some Tales of Local Color from Southeast Alabama," *SFQ* 24 (1960), 147–156.
Browne, Ray B. "Negro Folktales from Alabama," *SFQ* 28 (1954), 129–134.
———. "Some Notes on the Southern Holler," *JAF* (1954), 73–77.
———. "Two Alabama Nonsense Orations," *SFQ* 17 (1953), 213–215.
Figh, Margaret Gillis. "Folklore in the Rufus Sanders Sketches," *SFQ* 19 (1955), 185–195.
———. "Jumping Jeremiah," *JAF* 63 (1950), 240.
———. "Nineteenth Century Outlaws in Alabama Folklore," *SFQ* 25 (1961), 126–135.
Kennedy, Renwick C. "Funeral Customs in the Alabama Black Belt, 1870–1910," *SFQ* 23 (1959), 169–171.
Mitcham, Mildred Bennett. "A Tale in the Making: The Face in the Window," *SFQ* 12 (1948), 241–257.

Nelson, Mildred M. "Folk Etymology of Alabama Place Names," *SFQ* 4 (1950), 193–214.

Penrod, James. "Minority Groups in Old Southern Humor," *SFQ* 22 (1958), 121–128.

_____. "Women in the old Southwestern Yarns," *Kentucky Folk Record* 1 (1955), 41–47.

Stroup, Thomas B. "Analogues to the MAK Story: *A Second Shepherd's Play* Alabama Folktale," *JAF* 47 (1934), 380–381.

Tartt, Ruby P. "Richard the Tall-Hearted: Alabama Sketches," *Southwest Review* 29 (1944), 234–244.

Terrell, Clemmie S. "Spirituals from Alabama," *JAF* 43 (1930), 322.

Altogether, folk-life studies in Alabama are more limited than those in folklore, but they are more numerous than we might expect considering the absence of any state commission or state-wide organization in folklore and folk life. The WPA folklore research in Alabama produced some studies in architecture on a county and town basis, and the WPA interviews conducted with former slaves are most fruitful sources for the study of antebellum Negro folk culture. Dr. Penrod organized and taught the first course in folklore at Troy State University during the early 1950s. The Alabama Historical Commission has issued one significant study of folk architecture, *Alabama Folk Houses*, by Eugene M. Wilson, 1975. Although the emphasis is on the architecture rather than the folk, the text is brief and readable and the photographs are very fine documents. A companion volume, issued by the Alabama Historical Commission, *Alabama Ante-Bellum Architecture*, 1976, deserves mention here because of its connection with another WPA agency closely related to the National Writer's Project. The Historic American Buildings Survey, like the American Guides series and the programs in music, theater, dance, and writing, was designed to provide employment for white-collar workers and to make an accurate, detailed, and complete record of America's historic buildings. HABS, one of the survivors of the vast machinery of the FERA and WPA, is now a division of the National Parks Service. In Alabama the directorship fell to E. Walter Burkhardt, who with the assistance of his wife prepared a series of newspaper articles and photographs for the Sunday magazine of the *Birmingham News-Age-Herald* over a four-year period. *Alabama Ante-Bellum Architecture*, which reprints the Burkhardt series, is devoted mainly to the great houses of Southern legend, but there are some photographs of schools, churches, and the homes of ordinary folk as well as local history and nuggets of folklore. The original Burkhardt photographs and documents are on deposit in the archives of the Historic American Buildings Survey at the Library of Congress.

The deficiencies in Alabama folklore scholarship and field research may be explained in terms of (1) the absence of folklore agencies and organizations through which research and publication would naturally be conducted, and (2) the dearth of folklore courses in Alabama colleges and universities. A preliminary survey indicates that the University of North Alabama offers one graduate course in American folklore; Lomax Hannon Junior College has one three-hour introductory course; The University of Alabama offers Appalachian folklore, popular ballads, folk dance, three hours of independent study, and an introductory course; Chattahoochee Valley and John C. Calhoun dropped their courses in folklore; Samford University offers American Folklore, Southern Folklore, American Dialect, European Origins of Folklore, and several other research courses; and Alexander City Junior College offers one course in methodology and field research. However, when we take into account the WPA collections in folk tales, slave narratives, and folk songs, folklore-history articles printed in *The Alabama Review* and *The Alabama Historical Quarterly*, scatterings of scholarly articles in the *Journal of American Folklore* and the *Southern Folklore Quarterly*, various historical, literary, and newspaper sources, the books by Julian Rayford and Carl Carmer, personal accounts in diaries and memoirs, the field studies made by Arnold, Courlander, Ramsey, and Dr. Browne, and the Lomax recordings for the Library of Congress, then the scope and variety in Alabama folklore scholarship is a bit more impressive than the Smith bibliography indicates. It is clear, however, that a current need exists in Alabama for the establishment of folklore organizations, of centers for folklore archives, or full college and university programs in folklore, and of an Alabama Commission on Folklore and Folk Life. We hope that our own efforts in *Cracklin Bread and Asfidity* and *Zickary Zan* will aid in the creation of those agencies that will encourage and support scholarship, field research, and publications in Alabama folklore and folk life.

★☆★☆★☆★☆★☆★☆★☆★☆★☆★☆★☆★☆★☆★☆★☆

Collecting: Old Times and New Friends

The gathering of verbal folklore—riddles and rhymes, games and proverbs—poses few problems for the amateur collector, and the rewards are far greater than the difficulties. If the collector is interested in the extended interview, or oral biography, many of these folklore items will turn up in the natural course of conversation. If the catalog or archives approach is better suited to your purposes, it will be necessary to contact many informants of varying ages, occupations, and interests. Children readily share their riddles, sayings, songs, and games, but it is a good idea to seek the permission of their adult guardians, teachers, and parents. You may wish to survey an entire school, from kindergarten to seniors. If so, explain your intent to the school administration, and seek the cooperation of teachers, clubs, and classes. For every informant, note name, age, and address. If you like, you may devise a simple questionnaire in which you ask where, how, when, and from whom the informant learned the game, rhyme, or riddle. Everybody likes to be thanked—write a note when you have completed your study; if the study is printed or circulated, list every informant; and whenever possible, provide a copy of your findings for your informants.

The only mechanical requirements are an inexpensive, reliable, portable tape recorder and a modestly priced, simple-to-operate camera. Photographs, sketches, and taped recordings of conversations will enrich your study; but you can do all sorts of things with just paper, pen, or pencil, if you bring time, energy, and sincerity to your collecting projects. Individual field study is fine; collecting with family and friends is even better, not only because you can cover a broader territory but because of the agreeable, friendly companionship your folklore jaunts will bring. It helps to have a friend carry the picnic basket, drive the car, take photographs, or sketch. If your project is really big, find a sponsoring organization willing to provide minimal funds for paper, film, gasoline, and publishing—the PTA, the town or county historical association, local garden, literary, and civic clubs.

Don't overlook written sources. Attics, old trunks, and basements may yield treasures: letters, diaries, journals, and old newspapers may contain fine specimens of verbal folklore, and always these documents provide a splendid sense of folk life. Start with your own family, then your neighbors. The scraps will accumulate rapidly, and before you know it, you'll have a sizable collection. If you are a history buff, you will concentrate on older informants, but you can also make excellent collections of contemporary folklore. T-shirt mottos and emblems, high school and college cheers, current jokes and puzzles, bumper stickers, C.B. jargon, and sidewalk graffiti all lend themselves to folklore gathering; and these areas are relatively scant in collection and study.

How to keep it all together? Some collectors use index cards and manila folders; some, large portfolios and shoe boxes. For years and years we kept ours in petticoat boxes saved for us by our merchant friend Buddy Moncrief. The best guideline is to devise whatever storage arrangements, classifications, and filing systems are suited to your own needs and personality. Don't ever throw anything away! Every stage of your study, from the first tentative jottings to the final form, ought to be saved. Don't lend anything out unless you are positive that you have another copy. As your collection grows and you deepen your knowledge of folklore, as your awareness of the folk spirit sharpens, you will alter your methods of classification and your filing systems. A project you once believed would take two weeks may take a year, and a grandiose scheme may fizzle to one folder. If you need and can afford it, a filing cabinet will provide storage of photographs, sketches, drawings, tapes and cassettes, all "paper" items, and supplies. Heavy-duty cardboard boxes, arranged according to the physical nature of your materials or the kinds of folklore you are collecting (tales, songs, interviews, the supernatural, childlore) will do just as well.

The collection of artifacts, anything from farm implements to cooking utensils and folk toys, is another matter. If a craftsman whom you have interviewed for several times should give you some token or sample of his work, honor his generosity and friendship by your acceptance. Most artifacts, however, must be purchased. If you have money to spend, you can buy all sorts of folk artifacts at specialty shops, fairs, and festivals. Arts-and-crafts fairs, folk-music jamborees, and bazaars are flourishing everywhere. Remember that what you find here may be a commercial exploitation of our newly discovered interest in the past, though often you can enjoy very fine authentic folk items and craftsmen at these fairs without spending a penny. A small collection of artifacts gathered over the years from various informants will be a cherished possession, a happy reminder of the folk who shared their skills, memories, and lives with you. That the artifacts have little monetary value is irrelevant; it is their value as symbols of folk life that matters. Nor need the collections of these artifacts be a conscious search: many of the people you consult for riddles, rhymes, and games will be quite willing for you to duplicate or photograph both verbal lore and material folk items. Children, in particular, are always happy to oblige collectors with drawings and crayon sketches of their games, rhymes, and jokes.

After you exhaust family, friends, and neighbors, what next? How do you find more informants? Word-of-mouth. Once a few folks know you are interested in these matters, word will fly. We can almost guarantee that, in a short time, you will have located enough informants to last a year. Schools, churches, stores, community gathering places, organizations of farmers, retired schoolteachers, ex GI's, baseball and football players—all these will help you satisfy your inquiries.

Finally, the spirit of folklore excludes all patronizing attitudes. Other than the friends made along the way, the greatest reward of folklore collecting is the respect we develop for folk cultures other than our own. At first, you may be a bit put out when you spend four hours and have nothing to show for it but a handful of rhymes and a skinned ankle. After awhile you will come to understand that you brought home one riddle and a thousand invisible ties to old times and new friends.

Acknowledgments

Our thanks go to

The staff of the Thomas D. Russell Library of Alexander City State Junior College, especially Mrs. Carolyn Ingram, Mrs. Joyce Robinson, Mrs. Eula Hardaway, Mrs. Peggy Causey, and Mrs. Frances Tapley; and to those librarians, wherever they are, who answered our calls for help, especially Dr. Ruth Fourier of the Ralph Draughon Library of Auburn University for her continued encouragement, faith, and prompt action.

Brenda Croley, Phyllis Hornsby, Marrell McNeal, Freddy Langford, Chris Harris, and Allen Guy who labored with us.

Dr. W. Byron Causey, president of Alexander City State Junior College, and Dr. Charles Farrow, dean of the faculty, Alexander City State Junior College, for their encouragement in the pursuit of this volume.

Mr. James Travis for valuable editorial assistance and suggestions.

Miss Sarah Scott for her musical notations of the game songs.

Children, both then and now, who have played these games, sung these rhymes, and joyfully kept these things alive.

Contributors

Allen, Ella Kate
Allen, Pauline
Brown, Patricia
Brown, Patti
Brown, Yvonne
Burton, Bessie (Stanfield)
Burton, Bob
Burton, Ella (Roton)
Burton, Jim
Burton, Joe
Burton, Kate (Herren)
Burton, Lucy (Woodell)
Burton, Maggie (Story)
Burton, Minnie (Harwell)
Burton, Ruth (Herren)
Campbell, Estelle
Canales, Duane
Carroll, Mrs. Louis
Cauley, Willie Dora
Colquett, Cecilia
Conner, Carolyn
Cottle, Duffy
Davis, Lonnie D.
Delony, Linda
Duncan, Clyde
Evans, Johnny
Fannin, Joe
Formby, M. S.
Gavin, Maylene
Geiger, Eloise H.
Geiger, Rebecca
Gibson, Bascom
Goolsby, Bill
Gregory, Peggy

Ham, Mrs. James H.
Hayes, J. P.
Hebr, Fannie
Hicks, Mary Glenn
Hinton, Gayla
Hornsby, Jim
Hornsby, Ruth Herren
Hudson, Ophelia
Hughes, Mrs. Randolph
Jackson, Miss Mollie
Maddox, Charles
Medley, Mrs. James
Merritt, Mary Glenn
Messick, Cumy
Messick, Lurlene
Moore, Kathryn
Nelson, Carolyn
Patterson, Levon (Buddy), Jr.
Pearce, Tod
Pearson, J. M.
Pemberton, Little
Perryman, Hattie
Pienezza, Mackie
Richardson, Caroline
Richardson, Charles
Snell, Tullulah
Sutton, Susie
Turner, Carolyn
Turner, Earnest
Traweek, Jimmy
Walker, Jacob
White, Sylvia
Wilkerson, Mrs. Howell
Wilson, Ethylene